M AYSE YOUNG was born Mayse Dowling in 1913 in northern Queensland. She grew up in outback camps until, in 1929, her family bought the Pine Creek Hotel in the Northern Territory. In 1933, she married Joe Young and between 1934 and 1952 she had eight children. While bringing up her family, she continued to run the Pine Creek and Katherine Hotels. Today, she is a great-grandmother.

G ABRIELLE DALTON was born in Griffith, NSW in 1953, and completed an Honours Arts degree at the University of Sydney in 1975. She has worked as a journalist, arts administrator, film producer and writer and has travelled extensively throughout Australia. She is married with two children.

MAYSE YOUNG
WITH GABRIELLE DALTON

No Place
for a Woman

— ~ —

The autobiography of
Outback publican, Mayse Young

PAN
AUSTRALIA

First published 1991 by Pan Macmillan Publishers Australia
a division of Pan Macmillan Australia Pty Limited
63-71 Balfour Street, Chippendale, Sydney
Reprinted 1991 (three times), 1992

National Library of Australia
cataloguing-in-publication data:

Young, Mayse, 1913-   .
No place for a woman.

ISBN 0 330 27235 7

1. Young, Mayse, 1913- . 2. Hotelkeepers – Northern Territory – Biography. I.
Dalton, Gabrielle. II. Title.

647.940092

Typeset in Andover, by Post Typesetters
Printed in Australia by The Book Printer
Designed by Dimitrios Frangoulis

The photographs in this book are from the Mayse Young Collection.

Front cover images: Mayse Dowling in 1932, against the background of the
Pine Creek Hotel.
Cover design based on a concept by Gabrielle Dalton

To the memory of my parents, Evelyn and George Dowling and my brother, Ted.

CONTENTS

Foreword by Tom Cole   ix

Introduction   xi

I

1974: A Shattered Christmas   1

II

1913–1927: Home in a Tent   5

III

1927: Across the Barkly into the Never Never   23

IV

1929: Our Great Overland Trek   37

V

1929–1931: New Publicans at Pine Creek   55

VI

1931–1933: Life Goes on at Pine Creek   75

VII

1933–1942: Back to Camp Fire Cooking   91

VIII

1942–1945: The War Years   109

IX

1945–1952: Starting Again   119

X

1952–1959: Katherine   131

XI
1959–1963: Into my Mother's Shoes   145

XII
1963–1974: Hazards Natural and Unnatural   157

XIII
1974: No Quiet Retirement   169

Postscript   177

FOREWORD

IT WAS WITH A great deal of pleasure that I received a request to write the foreword to *No Place for a Woman*.

I first met Mayse in 1929, shortly after her family arrived in the tiny Northern Territory mining town of Pine Creek. The Dowling family had made the brave decision to take over the only hotel.

I would come in from the buffalo camps, ride up to the hotel, tie my horse up to the marvellous old shady tree at the side and join my friends there.

During the 1930s, Pine Creek was a hive of industry with miners and prospectors coming north to escape the Depression. I might add that this still meant that there was about one soul to every 500 square miles. However, they all homed in on the Pine Creek Hotel.

The Dowling family had made the hotel most hospitable and their daughter Mayse had the most delightful, bright personality. She always had a happy word for everybody and there was always a marvellous amount of good humour in the hotel. If things got a bit too jovial, Mayse could control the rowdiest gathering of miners with just a few words.

At the time I thought she was the most beautiful young woman I had ever seen — everybody loved her. The respect with which Mayse and her mother were treated is rarely seen today.

Many years later I renewed my friendship with Mayse. By then she had become an outstandingly successful business woman. Her interests now are wide and varied and she is still active overseeing her many investments in the Northern Territory.

She can look back on a rich pioneering life of great success and many friends.

Tom Cole, Sydney 1991

INTRODUCTION

IN 1985, I was working in the Northern Territory researching *Frontier Women*, a film about the remarkable women of the outback.

People throughout the Territory had spoken to me of Mayse Young, who had owned and run the Pine Creek Hotel for many years. She was sitting on the cool vine-covered veranda of the hotel on a humid April afternoon, when I found her and I liked her immediately.

Although she was in her seventies, it was easy to see the renowned beauty she had been in her youth. She had a softness about her face and a gentle, almost shy manner — which surprised me as I knew she had experienced so much tough life in the outback.

We saw each other frequently over the next few months and as we got to know each other our friendship grew. We would often talk about Mayse's early experiences. I was fascinated by the abandoned corrugated-iron building which had been the original Pine Creek Hotel and loved to walk down there with Mayse, encouraging her to reminisce about the place as it was when she and her family first arrived to take it over in 1929.

I said to her, 'You know, you should write all this down — it would make a wonderful book!'

I was thinking of how many other people would enjoy her stories, her bush sense of humour and the inspiring courage with which she had tackled and overcome the many disasters in her life.

When I called in to the Pine Creek Hotel, to say

goodbye to Mayse before heading south, I handed her a large empty notebook, and said to her jokingly, 'This is my challenge to you, to start the book we talked about!'

Nearly a year later, I received in the mail a parcel from Pine Creek. It contained the notebook, every page filled with flowing handwriting, and a note saying, 'How do you think I'm going? Mayse.'

I was thrilled with what I read. From then on, we worked in earnest. We were half a continent away from each other, so we communicated by mail and telephone, meeting when we could. Finally, at the end of several years of working — interrupted by the birth of my son and daughter — we have had the satisfaction of completing *No Place for a Woman*. We hope you will enjoy it.

Gabrielle Dalton, 1991

Darwin
Pine Creek
Katherine
Derby
Wave Hill
Broome
Fitzroy
Crossing
Halls Creek
Port Hedland
Marble Bar
Innisfail
Ingham
Tully
1927
Camooweal
Mt Isa
Duchess
Proserpine
Winton
Meekatharra
Brisbane
Geraldton
Coolgardie
1929
Port Augusta
Crystal Brook
Perth
Norseman
Sydney
Adelaide
Melbourne

Approximate scale in miles
0   250   500

The journeys of the Dowling family 1927–1929

· I ·

1974: A SHATTERED CHRISTMAS

Darwin, first light on Christmas morning, 1974.
I waded out through knee-deep water, across what had been our
loungeroom floor. Among the shattered glass and sodden
furniture were scraps of Christmas tinsel, and just one
pathetic little package still in Merry Christmas wrapping,
caught in a tangle of splinters and broken fibro cement. The
unopened gifts we had placed with love and laughter under
the tree the night before had been blown or washed away in
fragments. Behind the Seabreeze Hotel, only one wall of the
manager's flat remained standing and we could see now that
this barrier certainly had saved our lives.
Standing in the unnatural silence and thick, humid heat, I found
myself struggling to believe the scene of destruction before me.
Only yesterday this had been our comfortable family hotel,
with its tropical beer garden overlooking East Point and the
Arafura Sea. Now, the hotel building was an unrecognisable
ruin, the garden had been stripped bare, the trees were
uprooted and the pool overflowed with smashed timber,
twisted iron, and a mass of sodden debris...

•

CYCLONE TRACY hit Darwin virtually
without warning, just after midnight. Winds of a
velocity of 217 kilometres per hour were measured at
the airport, before they destroyed the recording apparatus at 3.05 am and we were told later that the gusts
were estimated to have exceeded 250 kilometres per
hour. The Seabreeze Hotel received the full impact as
the cyclone blasted in across the Arafura Sea.

The terrifying screech of the cyclone pierced the
darkness as we huddled under mattresses. I held my

grandchildren tight to me, my mind focused on keeping them safe, and praying that it would stop before we were all killed. The storm seemed to go on and on endlessly, and then, to our immense relief, a lull came. Within twenty minutes however, the cyclone made a hairpin turn at sea and came roaring in at us again for several more hours before it finally passed.

When daylight came there was a deadly hush over the city, a shocked silence as people struggled to comprehend what had happened. We would learn later that ninety per cent of all the houses in Darwin were either completely destroyed or unliveable; sixty-five people were killed, and over one thousand injured. My home, our possessions and our hotel were all gone. I could see only irretrievable wreckage. There was no thought of Christmas Day celebrations now; that we were alive and unhurt was all that seemed to matter for the moment.

We walked through the wreckage in a daze, hardly speaking to one another, exhausted and overwhelmed. I picked my way through the remains of the hotel building. What had been the bar was a mass of shattered glass and splintered wood. In the kitchen, the refrigerators had been blown over and rolled around the room by the wind. Our Christmas hams and turkeys were already inedible in the heat, strewn across the floor.

One sight after another reinforced my gratitude that we had been sheltering in the manager's flat behind the main hotel building. My car, which had been parked out in front of the hotel, had been rolled over several times by the wind and now stood up on its side, a ghastly symbol of our overturned reality. The windows were shattered and it had been completely 'sandblasted' in the storm — stripped of all its duco.

Around us, there was not one house left standing in the eerie silence. Had any of these families survived? There was no sign of life, no one moving about in the jumble of wreckage, just row upon row of what looked like stacks of rubbish and timber, as far as I could see. The day before there had been a comfortable suburb, and leafy green streets full of the sound of children playing — now I saw a whole neighbourhood razed to the ground.

I wondered where all those people could have sheltered, where they had gone. An uncontrollable wave of emotion swept over me, and I started to weep. 'Why cry now, Mum?' my girls asked, 'It's all over.'

'But where are all the children?' I cried.

Struck by the vulnerability of all young ones who had suffered a night of unexpected terror, the fears and emotions I had held in check during the night rolled out of me in an exhausted few minutes of sobbing, while my daughters stood with their arms around my shoulders.

I had stood like this with my own mother, twenty-nine years earlier, outside the ruined shell of our family hotel in Pine Creek. In 1945 we had driven over three thousand miles, relieved the Second World War was finally over, joyous at the prospect of returning to the Territory. We stepped out of the truck to find the Pine Creek Hotel gutted and empty. Mum had broken down and cried then, too.

The next day however, she was her usual strong self and set us all the challenge of restoring the hotel to the comfortable haven it had been to the little outback town. She had inspired me to face the wreckage of my own home in Darwin after the Japanese bombing attacks had forced our evacuation.

'Material things can be replaced,' she had said. And they were.

Five days after Cyclone Tracy destroyed Darwin, I sat at the airport with my daughters and grandchildren, among hundreds of other women and children — Darwin's refugees. I needed my mother's strength and courage as never before. Could we start from nothing again?

3   1974: A Shattered Christmas

· II ·

1913–1927: HOME IN A TENT

MY FIRST MEMORIES of my early life were the canvas walls of our tent, my mother cooking over an open fire, and the satisfying taste of fresh baked damper with dripping, pepper and salt, or golden syrup.

My father was a lifting ganger with the railways in Queensland and it meant we were always moving. We would set up our camp just out of some little town, usually surrounded by the magnificent, unspoilt rainforests of the north. The lush green, the smells of damp undergrowth, the gigantic trees rising above us, the waterfalls and creeks in which we played, are the rich backgrounds to my childhood in the tropics.

New railway lines were being built all over north Queensland during the early 1920s. The railways were replacing the horse and bullock teams, and were a way of opening up the country to help the smaller towns and the farmers. They also provided employment for the returned men of the First World War.

Building railways was hard yakka then. Every shovelful of dirt and gravel that went into the foundations was moved by the gangs. Every sleeper was hand-cut; from the felling of the trees, to hauling the logs, sawing them into lengths, trimming them with adzes, and boring them with holes. Then they were laid out on the gravel foundations — all by manual effort.

The men carried the steel lengths of railway line from the wagons to be set side by side along the sleepers. Even the 'dogs' that were hammered through the rim of the railway line into the sleepers were hand-turned.

Dad and his team followed the plate-layers, as the builders were called. His gang was the lifting gang, and their function was to pound and pack the gravel and soil under the sleepers, and set the railway lines firm and straight, ready for the trains to travel over.

Rain or shine, hell or high water, Dad went to work every morning on the railways. He was told which railway construction camp needed gangers, and it was up to him to get himself there, at his own expense if he wanted the job. He would pack up our camp, along with mother and children, and travel by horse and wagon fifty or perhaps a hundred miles to the next job site.

As a small child, the effort of getting from one job to another didn't affect me. Life was running around the camp, having fun, three feeds a day, a bed to sleep in and Mum and Dad always there for me.

Home was a couple of canvas tents with make-shift tables and benches to sit on; it all seemed comfortable enough to me. Each time we moved there were dozens of things to be done around the new camp to make it liveable — clearing the grass, raking it over, then dampening the dust with water to lay it. Dad put wishbone-shaped poles into the ground to hold up a length of hessian for our beds. We all had our own jobs: setting up the cooking fire, carrying water, hobbling the horses, making the bush shower.

Our camp was always clean. The all-purpose utensil was the four-gallon petrol tin. They made shelves and the washing-up dish; with wire for handles they made boilers for the clothes and washing troughs and even our shower. The tin was pierced with nails and pulled up by a rope. The idea was to pour water into the tin and have a quick shower — the length depended on the number of nail holes! It was great, but you had to be quick. The bathroom was hessian bags nailed around four posts, or a couple of saplings that might just be growing close together. A box made up for the purpose placed over another petrol tin was our toilet.

I had never seen my mother cook on anything but an open fire. She had an iron-framed stool over the coals to stand the billy on, or two pieces of railway line propped on stones — the pots and pans were black. She boiled the clothes in a kerosene tin over an open fire; she made bread and damper in a camp oven buried deep in the ashes and red-hot coals. She would pin her skirt up to keep the hem away from the fire and often commented she had no hairs on her legs, because they were always singed off.

We were used to seeing her work like this: it was our way of life. I can't remember her ever complaining about her lot, or being cranky. Her competent, energetic presence always made us feel secure, and she made wherever we camped home. She would gently lay her hand on my shoulder if she saw me looking shy or sad; often she would just walk up and stand behind me, and gently stroke my hair.

She was a very special person, our mum. She had married George Dowling, my father, taken on his itinerant lifestyle, adapted to this nomadic way of living in temporary camps and given birth to me by the time she was sixteen.

•

Only when Dad had a job near a town was I able to go to school. I remember the first one I attended at South Johnstone. It was very small, built on stilts in the Queensland style and I hated it. Perhaps it was because I had a hate on my step-brother, George, at the time. George was much older, his mother was Dad's first wife and she had died in childbirth.

If George had to babysit me he would take me into a corn or cane field, flatten out a spot, and leave me there until he returned. Those corn stalks seemed to be twelve feet high, and the cane even higher. It was very frightening when you were only little and had a fear of rats, frogs, and snakes. To get to school, we had to cross the South Johnstone River bridge, stepping from railway sleeper to railway sleeper, trying not to look at the water far below us. If the river was in flood, George would bunch my skirt at the back and push me along. This always made me feel more afraid of the swirling water beneath me than if he had let me step across at my own pace.

The only teacher at this school suffered epileptic fits. The first time it happened was a shocking thing for the pupils, I can tell you. He made a roaring noise like a wild bull, kids jumped out of windows, over the balcony, or ran down the stairs. We little ones were on the veranda, so we were the first down those stairs. He must have cut himself when he fell to the floor of the classroom, hitting his head, because blood was dripping through the floorboards on to the cement below. While the bigger boys ran for help we just stood and stared in horror at the growing red pool. After this first time, he showed the older boys what to do if it happened again. Each time we would have the rest of the day off. I must confess that I wished he would have a fit every school day. He never had enough as far as I was concerned.

I must have been a real bush kid, because I can remember my first experience of a telephone. It was in South Johnstone, where the local shop was the local everything — including post office. One day I was in the shop alone, when the owner said, 'Just stay here for a minute, I've got to pop outside.' While I was waiting, the telephone rang — it was one of those wall jobs — and I took the handle off the hook, as I had seen the lady do, and put it up to my ear. When a voice seemed to come from no-where, and yelled 'Hello' at me, I dropped the handset and took off, running for dear life, not stopping until I was well and truly home: as far as I was concerned, 'it was properly debbil, debbil,' as the old blackfellows would say.

When our baby brother Jim was born at Home Hill, a small town in the north of Queensland, Mum went into a nursing home. I went along with my other brother, Ted, who was eighteen months younger than I. We were both very shy, lonely and frightened, and on top of that we had sandy blight. We felt that our eyes were full of sand. They were all red and puffed up, and the lids would stick together. They had to be bathed with Epsom salts or cold tea to make them open again.

The nurse would get us up in the morning, bathe our eyes, feed us, then put us outside. Most of the time we spent crying at the screen door, or huddled together under a shady tree in the back yard. We were glad to go home to our tent.

We had a long stay at Silkwood. My sister Ethel was born there on the day Poitrel won the Melbourne Cup. She was tiny and cried a lot. Our mother had to express milk from Ethel's little breasts each morning then put a tight binder around her chest, an old fashioned method used to dry up the milk which formed in some babies' breasts. The baby would cry, Mother would cry, and Ted and I would cling to each other down in the yard, usually behind the dunny for some unknown reason — perhaps it was as far as we were game to go from the tent — and cry too.

Later, there were happier times at Silkwood. Sometimes we would go into the deep cool forests to look for wild raspberries or guavas. If Mum put red pants on our baby brother, Jim, we would take them off and lie them on the grass to attract the beautiful Blue Mountain butterflies; they were magic creatures to us.

My happiest school memories were of Innisfail. We had a teacher who was great fun; she taught us to spell words by putting them into song. I still have to sing to spell words like 'Indooroopilly' and 'ornithorhynchus'.

Some mornings, on our way to school, the butcher would hand out a raw sausage to eat — it wasn't bad! And after school we would wander into the little general store run by a Chinese family, to look at the goodies before playing down at the creek where we drank water from the cunjevoi leaves.

The rain forests were beautiful. The quandong and damson trees were my favourites, next to the ginger and wild plums. I loved the running streams, and the damp and musty smell of the bracken. I would spend hours just lying around in the ferns, daydreaming.

We had a light wagon, two beautiful grey draught horses called Barnie and George, who were the leaders, and several other horses. Dad had purchased a little chestnut pony for me, and I called him Tiny. He was so quiet you could go to sleep on his back (which I often did). If I fell off he would just stand and wait for me to remount.

When we were on the move, my job was spareboy, which meant I tailed, or rode behind the horses which were not harnessed that day. At daybreak I had to help round them up. After a while I could tell where they were from the tone of their Condamine bells. I can still recall standing in the cool early morning mist and listening to the sweet tinkling sound.

When we set out for a new camp, the wagon was loaded with folded tents, swags, tucker, boxes, our home-made utensils, the dog, a cocky and a coop with a few hens. Hurricane lamps, water bags and rope hung on the sides. It was little wonder when we set up camp at a small creek in one little town that a kid driving a billy-goat cart came down to ask when the circus was opening!

From Mackay we drifted up the coast. Proserpine I remember, because of the number of water snakes at the waterhole. Some evenings, Mum and Dad would have a competition to see who could shoot the most. Mum handled the gun with confidence, and she had as good an aiming eye as Dad, so she would often come out the winner. Their catch would be strung over the fence, and sometimes there would be up to twenty snakes, much to the delight of their children, the eager spectators.

In Proserpine, before the cane-cutting began, the cane beetles came in swarms. At night, we would put down a white groundsheet with a hurricane lamp in the middle, and then shake the tree. The light attracted the beetles and we would gather them into four-gallon petrol tins. The farmers paid us one pound a tin.

We younger ones had treacle tins and we would get two and sixpence for each one filled with the coloured beetles. We made quite a lot of money during the season, but we had sore fingers. The beetles clung to our fingers with their sharp little legs and had to be pulled off.

We ate well in these lush farmland areas. Pineapples were cheap, there were farms where you could eat as many as you liked for sixpence. We just cut them in half and ate them with a spoon . . . they were delicious. You could 'hire' fruit trees for five shillings for the season, and all the fruit on that tree was yours — mandarins, oranges, grapefruit, and pomelos.

At Ingham school we would sit on the grass under a tree in the garden and chant 'times' tables. I had never been close to a real garden of flowers before, and it fascinated me. I spent hours watching the bees disappearing down the throat of a snapdragon, and smelling the sweet sultry perfumes. I also remember hanging over the school fence and, not knowing quite why, chanting nonsense like 'Catholic dogs jump like frogs, and don't eat meat on Fridays!' at the pupils from the other school.

One terrifying night a curlew ran under my

bunk. The cry of the curlew and the howl of dingoes always makes my blood run cold. That night, it could have been a swamp Banksia — bogeyman — for all I knew. I just sat huddled in the dark, too scared to move.

We were camped a few miles out of town. By this time Mum had a buggy and an ex-racehorse (so she said), called Paddy. She drove us to school each day in the sulky. I wasn't sure if it was due to Paddy's yearnings for the racetrack, or his temperamental behaviour when he refused to be harnessed up to the sulky, but it was here that we acquired our first motor car.

It was a Dodge. A snake would have broken its back following the wheel tracks when our mother was learning to drive. One day when she couldn't catch Paddy, she drove into town to pick us up at school. As she hadn't yet learned to reverse, she had to make a very wide circle of the town to get back home!

•

TULLY, OR BANYAN as it was known then, was our next home. We camped on the bank of the Banyan River, but as I recall, we ended up spending quite a bit of our time in the local blacksmith's shop each time the river came down in flood. Like fowls to roost, that's where the Dowlings, along with several other families, always took refuge. It was the highest and driest place in town. Dad would swim down to our camp each day to check our belongings and usually found our bits and pieces floating around inside the tent.

The Banyan River flowed into the Tully River and on towards the magnificent Tully Falls, where we often went on picnics. This is the most beautiful place in my memories of north Queensland. The rainforest trees were immense, making us feel like tiny creatures in a giant's garden, but I felt comfortable and happy under the lush green canopy, among the misty undergrowth of ferns and sweet mossy smells. It always seemed to be raining, but it was warm tropical rain, with brilliant, hot, sunny periods between the cloud bursts. So when we got wet, we didn't bother to change clothes — they were soon dry again. We had a saying here that it rained for nine months of the year, and then the wet season set in! Rainfall was measured in feet, not inches.

We stayed at Tully for about two years, and it was here that I had my longest stretch of schooling. It was routine that I got the cane every day because I didn't know my tables. The way to school was a path through the sugar cane mill. The juicy sugar cane was a treat; and it accounted for all the bee stings — there were swarms of bees everywhere — and all the trips to the dentist. Both were so painful that they are indelible memories. The dentist used one of the old treadle drills, he pedalled like mad with one foot and had a drill like a crow bar, and just as blunt. There was no anaesthetic and how it hurt!

I learnt to swim in the Banyan River. I rigged up some old tins, tied a bone to the bottom for bait and a string to the handle to anchor it to a stone or log. After school each day, I would sit on the bank day-dreaming. Periodically I would dive in and get my catch of yabbies. My two pet white ducks wandered down to the riverbank from our camp, so I would hunt through the grass, looking for their eggs.

Around the bottoms of the pylons of the Banyan River Bridge were deep wash-outs, forming an eddy. One afternoon, I saw a girl get caught in one of these. She was bobbing up and down and couldn't get out. I plunged in and managed to pull her to safety. After vomiting up half the river, she looked white and shaken, so I helped her home. Her mother came out, took one look, grabbed her by the arm and began scolding her about going near the river. No thank-you to me. I guess I was lucky not to get a box on the ears as well!

My friend Flossie, whose parents owned a farm out from Tully, had a couple of nasty little brothers who rolled around on the ground laughing each time I visited. I had told them my mother said that ducks laid their eggs from under their wings! One day they put me on a frisky pony and it bolted into town. It only stopped when it reached the post office. Perhaps this was its usual run. Anyway I stayed on all the way, with my arms wrapped around its neck and hat trailing a yard behind my head, the elastic under my chin nearly choking me. They were a rough mob! I learned to ride a pushbike in Tully, too. Mum bought me an old boys' bike, and for the first couple of weeks I was the scabbiest kid in town.

Then we sold our wagon and horses, and Dad bought an old Ford truck. I learnt to drive about this time — I was nine years old. A workmate of Dad's would take Ted and me out in the truck and let us drive in the bush. Left alone in the front seat, while he sat on the tray of the truck at the back smoking his pipe, we just had to work things out for ourselves. If you didn't give it enough juice and stalled going up a hill, you just rolled back down to the bottom and started again. There would be a patient silence from our teacher on the back.

Dad worked on the Tully sugar mill trains. Now he was a riding ganger, one of the pair of men who would work the lever up and down on the pumper or quad car, which travelled the railway line. The pumper would take the men up or down the line, from their camp to where they worked. The boss of the group was called the ganger, and the men the lizards; the lizards and the ganger got to ride to work, sitting in a line on each side of the pumper, their feet dangling down the sides.

Mum set up our tent-home and made a garden and we loved it. Tassel ferns grew on logs, there were wild orchids and tree ferns, staghorns and crows nests, passionfruit vines and granadillas. We nibbled the stems of sourcops. In the scrub we found wild tomatoes, raspberries, guavas, conker berries, and damsons, wild plums and ginger. In our cubby house we nailed the fast-growing plant of life everywhere, and around each leaf grew little bushes and mobs of roots; even the coleus grew nailed to a post.

It was hard to leave. We had made friends at school, and we had learned to mix with other kids. Once, I had to be prodded from under the bed when anyone called to visit; now I ventured out and hid behind Mum's skirt! After leaving Tully we went to Mt Molloy, outside Mareeba. This was timber country with sawmills that stood out in the towns, but Dad still worked on the railways.

I liked the Mt Molloy school much better. We had a lovely lady teacher, and for the first time I felt part of a group outside my family. I must have been growing up. The teacher would call to the class, 'Stand straight, put your chest out, march like Mayse!' This left me red-faced, and I developed round shoulders. I could out-run and out-jump the other kids in my class, and got into more trouble than Speed Gordon for playing football with the boys, a definite 'no' for young ladies then.

I was now eleven, going on twelve, and it was here that I got my first pair of shoes: Mum chose button-up boots for me, because she believed that they were good for my ankles. It was strange wearing shoes after so many years of running around barefoot, but I felt really grown-up. It was at this time that I fell in love for the first time. He was the postmaster's son. Mind you, I can't even remember that the light of my life ever spoke to me. Then the school announced a fancy-dress afternoon. My first-ever party!

I was allowed to choose my own costume so, out to impress the postmaster's son who still wouldn't speak to me, I decided to become a hula dancer. Mother even arranged for a lady to make me some red paper roses. Finally, the big day came. My skirt was brown crêpe paper cut into strips, but I had to wear it over my white frock, which had puff sleeves and a collar, and with my white socks and black ankle boots. I had a ribbon around my neck, from which hung the two big red paper roses and a rose in my hair!

I arrived full of excitement and anticipation. Then I saw my rival, talking to the postmaster's son. The humiliation. There she was, also dressed as a hula girl. But she had bare brown legs, a skimpy top, a lei around her neck, anklets and armlets, and a dirty big smirk! The boys pulled bits off my skirt all afternoon, and I went home feeling ashamed, and looking very bedraggled, and definitely *off* the postmaster's son.

It was a touchy time for me. I even ran away from home — my first and last attempt. I don't think I had a good reason for this. I sat on my little swag but no one ever came down that track near our tents. Mum and Dad must have known where I was, and thought it best to let me work it out on my own for a while. So I sat in the twilight feeling thoroughly miserable. When it got dark and I got hungry, I gave up and went home.

These were to be the last of my school days, which troubled me. I still wanted to learn. But as with all our other schools, we only stayed for a short time, and in a few months we moved on, and my formal schooling was over forever. I was twelve years old.

•

WE DRIFTED westward across to Cloncurry. It was a long and interesting trip. We camped on the banks of flooded creeks, and sat for hours watching the stick in the ground at water level, waiting to see if the river was still coming up, or going down. Finally, the beautiful rain forests with their cool clear rivers and streams were behind us and we travelled the hot dry outback with its red dust, dry creek beds and flies.

When we pulled into Winton, in central-west

Queensland, we marvelled at the artesian bore. We swam where the water was lukewarm, and watched the boiling bore water gush up from underground. It was an incredible sight to see the billy tea made without having to light a fire, and corned beef strung on a piece of wire cook right through in the water.

At Cloncurry we set up camp in a dry creek bed. When we went into town, Mum let us have a soft drink — and it was a treat indeed! Oh, the terrible decision I had to make when choosing a cola or a raspberry. We sat down to drink it, feeling very sophisticated, in a little shop with tables and chairs.

I had my thirteenth birthday while we were at Cloncurry, and Mum bought some boiled lollies and soft drinks back to the camp so we could have a little family party. For my present I was given some money to buy myself a gift. I had never shopped before, and it was scary. I told the lady in the shop, 'I want a pair of stockings for a friend . . . about my size . . . ' I had no idea what colour. I also wanted lipstick. 'Colour?' 'Red!' I did show the stockings to my mother, but as she had never used makeup in her life, I wasn't game to bring out the lipstick! Anyhow, it melted in the heat, and ran into my purse. So I never did use it, but it smelt good! As it was always too hot to wear stockings, they proved a dead loss as well, but it was nice just looking at them and pretending.

The day we arrived at Duchess, someone had stolen the safe from the local pub. The place was humming with excitement, and we children were thrilled by all the drama. By the time the safe was found blown open and emptied down at the dump a few days later, the thieves were long gone and probably still going!

Dad started work on the railway construction that was linking Duchess to Mt Isa. We soon had the tents up and made a lean-to for shade with whatever we could scrounge: bits of iron, bags, anything to give shelter.

The pride of our camp was our old gramophone: it gave out a hauntingly beautiful sound in the bush. Mother loved music and used to sing to us a lot, and this was her one and only luxury. We children loved it. We often had family singalongs, and Dad would always ask me to sing him his favourite songs, 'Wait 'Til The Clouds Roll By, Maggie' and 'White Wings'.

I remember Mum in those days as slim and good-looking. She had dark brown hair, which was very thick and waist-length. A Queensland doctor told her to have her hair cut, as the weight may have been causing her bad headaches. It took a long time for us to get used to Mum with short hair. She had a very placid nature, with a good sense of humour and often joined in our fun and games.

Not all the dancing and prancing about was done by Mum and the kids. Dad had told us that as a lad he was a contortionist and tightrope walker in a circus. His mother was Rose Ashton, from the Ashton Circus, and he and his brother Jim both performed until they took off and went their own ways, as he put it.

Dad was dark-haired and handsome, a slightly built man, but very agile. He was suntanned and fit from his outdoor work, and I always remember him with a cigarette holder in the corner of his mouth, with or without a smoke in it. He was quiet and gentle and very good-natured with us. When he had time off work, he liked having a bit of fun. He would draw a circle around his feet in the dust, leap up from the spot, do a double somersault and land back in the circle again, or turn and twist his body through a number of hoops — tricks learnt in his circus days.

We would watch in open-mouthed delight, as he rubbed places between the muscles on his leg or arm, and stuck pins into himself right down to their heads — he said it didn't hurt. He would also stick pins into his forehead, so they just hung there, and he would laugh at the reaction of his audience.

'The Duchess' wasn't much of a town, and the

flies nearly drove Mum crazy. How she managed I'll never know. There was always plenty of tucker, but getting it from plate to mouth was no mean feat. So, one day Dad built us a fly-proof hut! We stood back and admired it — a magic shed made of hessian. The opening was made of flaps overlapping for coming and going.

The blokes from the neighbouring camps admired it, and the only other woman gazed in envy. At meal times we would arm ourselves with branches and shoo like crazy, while Mum took in the food. We could all sit around the table: four posts in the ground, and planks along the top. It was heaven indeed, just too good to last.

We were getting used to this luxury when my little sister, playing with matches, burnt it down. Poor Mum, she couldn't believe her eyes. Nor could we! All black and smoking, the hessian hanging like cobwebs from the frames. One minute it was there and in just a few seconds gone!

So it was back to the meat safe for the kids! This was made of hessian too, but smaller, so we had to take it in turns to eat, or take our chances battling with the sticky bush flies outside.

•

JUST OUT FROM DUCHESS was the small town called Dajarra. It was the destination for all the droving plants (the men, horses and all their gear). They brought the big mobs of cattle in from the Kimberley and the Northern Territory — some travelling overland for up to six months — to get to the railhead.

We met our great-grandmother there. She was a tall, regal lady, much in contrast with the dusty outback nature of this little town. She made an indelible impression on me. Her long hair was still dark brown, coiled into a bun and, despite the heat, she wore a long black skirt and white high-necked blouse with long sleeves. We children were totally in awe of her. Great-grandmother Morgan we were told, had been born into a 'titled' family. She had left her fine home to marry Harry Morgan, a teamster — how and why was never explained and we were too much in awe of her to ask.

We only saw her once and she treated us to lunch in a rough, but real restaurant — the only one in town. To us, it was very grand. The four of us, dressed in our best and on our best behaviour, did our parents proud, I hope!

The hardships my great-grandmother must have endured in those early times would have been much tougher even than those in my mother's life. Besides the dust and flies, she had to bear the smell of working bullocks, travelling on the wagon over rough outback tracks and making only a few miles a day. Most of the time they slept under the stars, water came from the water bag, food from the tuckerbox, and there was no way of keeping anything cool. Bread was baked in the camp oven at night. And things were more difficult if they had children. But these outback women still wore their long dresses with dignity, sometimes with the skirt pinned up to keep the hem clean.

Fortunately we never seemed to have any ailments, we were a very healthy lot of kids. However, one day the other woman from the railway camp came to Mother in tears. Her baby had not wet her nappy for a couple of days. The child was fretful and ran a temperature. The nearest doctor was in Mt Isa, a two-day journey away. One part of our most treasured possessions was the old family doctor's book. Most outback people had one: it was like a bible. In this case, said the book of knowledge, take the seeds from a pumpkin (luckily spuds, onions and a sturdy old pumpkin were always in our larder), cover with water, and bring to the boil. Cool the liquid, and give to the patient to drink. Within no time at all it proved its worth! Happiness all round.

When the construction job from Duchess to Mt Isa finished, we moved our camp to Mt Isa, and stayed there for a while. At that time Mt Isa was a very small mining town. We spent Christmas of 1926 on the bank of a creek, just outside town.

I feel sure my parents never thought of moving to the Northern Territory until that Christmas, when Dad met someone in Mt Isa who told him of the railway line being built between Pine Creek and Birdum.

'It's a man's country,' he said, 'You'd be foolish to take a family up there. It's no place for a woman.'

When Dad discussed this remark with my mother, she pointed out that it couldn't be worse than the dry red earth, dust storms and flies around the Isa. Being a plucky soul, she was willing to take a chance. So, plans were made for the whole family to load up and travel to the Northern Territory.

· III ·

1927: ACROSS THE BARKLY INTO
THE NEVER NEVER

TO CROSS the barren Barkly Tableland
between Mt Isa and Darwin was a very dangerous undertaking in 1927. The only road was a dirt
track which followed the stock route; there would be
very few, if any other travellers on the track to help if
we were to get into trouble; and water holes were
scarce. We were warned that the heat, flies, mosquitoes, and sandflies were bad and that the water was
brackish and, in some cases, undrinkable. (We later
found the water as sweet as anywhere in Australia,
and heat, flies and mozzies are as Australian as corned
beef and beer anyway.)

Still, for a man to face the lonely bush road was one
thing; with Mum, four kids and all we owned packed on
to a one-ton truck, it was something else. The fact that
we planned to have two vehicles reassured my mother
that we would be fairly safe and that we wouldn't come
to a tragic ending out on the Barkly, like so many others
before us; also we had always been such healthy children, she did not anticipate any medical emergencies she
could not handle herself.

Dad planned that they would take the Dodge,
and Mum would drive it behind the truck so we had a
back-up. I often wonder what would have happened if
we had struck real trouble. I'm pretty sure Dad's
knowledge of what went on under the bonnet of a car
was limited.

We stocked the truck with tucker for the long trip, as well as fuel, our dog, cocky, chooks — and kids. My step-brother, George, had joined the family again for a while, so there were seven of us. We grew increasingly excited as the preparations were made. I was the only one who gleaned anything of the reservations being expressed about the trip, from the men who spoke to our father. But seeing Mum so confident stopped me entertaining any idea of dangers standing in our way.

We always carried a good supply of petrol in tins. My parents had the mileage and supply carefully worked out. It was important to have petrol, oil, grease, tyres and tubes, fan belts, spark plugs, and other spare parts that fixed the minor ailments of a vehicle. At last it was all packed, and we headed out on our great adventure soon after daylight one morning in February 1927.

Our first stop after Mt Isa was Camooweal. We would not pass through another town until we reached Katherine in the north, and we were expecting it to take us about three weeks to do the thousand-odd miles. We topped the load, and camped the night just out of town. The next morning we headed out across the endless flat plains of the Barkly. Our route would take us through Alexandria Downs, Brunette Downs, and Newcastle Waters Stations.

The travelling was rough and the days were long and frightening. We children had sobered up from our first excitement, and the fears felt by our parents — although they went unsaid — were now felt by us too. It felt very, very lonely out there; just our little family, with not even an animal in sight, day after day. We nursed the vehicles along, never pushing too fast, especially over the rough patches, averaging about fifty miles a day. One treeless plain was 125 miles wide — three days' travelling. We had to carry firewood, and water, and took care to check these supplies carefully each day before setting out.

As the 'road' was really a stock route, approximately every twenty-five miles we found a bore and windmill to water travelling stock. We played 'I spy the black dot' — which would be a windmill. From the time we lost sight of one windmill our eyes were searching the horizon for that dark spot that meant another one was coming up.

Mum was driving the car, and was a bit faster than Dad, who travelled at fifteen miles an hour flat out, come what may! She would get fed up and pull out ahead to set up the next camp, which pleased us if we were with her. We would wait at a gate or bore for him to catch up. This gave us a chance to stretch our legs. We would run up to the anthills, which were sometimes taller than we were and poke around in the low scrub for anything of interest. We collected any firewood we saw, always taking care never to stray too far from Mum and the car.

One afternoon Mum thought she would try Dad's shotgun. Being used to her little .22 rifle, she hadn't allowed for the recoil from the butt of the gun, and finished up lying on her back in the dust. After we had got over the fright, we all laughed. From then on she kept to the .22.

We slept under the stars in the dry weather, and it was only if the winds were strong and cold on the plains that Dad would build us a break of bushes or put up a tent. It was the rule to break camp early in the morning, and stop in plenty of time to bed-down before dark. There were always beds to make, firewood to be collected and perhaps a damper to be made. For a treat Mum would sometimes make Johnnie cakes on the coals. She would give us the dough to wrap around sticks, which we held in the fire until they were cooked. Then we ate them with syrup or jam — they were delicious!

If we came to a particularly nice camping spot we would take a day off from travelling and rest there. Mum caught up with her washing and baked a couple of extra dampers for the road; the boys and Dad filled all the water bags, and checked the cars. The old bath tub came off the truck, and we would have a good going-over — heads washed and all. Old Rover rushed around with excitement and chased all the crows and hawks that tried to come in for a drink — then parked himself under the truck to cool off. Cocky seemed to enjoy himself all the time, and the chooks were let out in the evening. They always returned to their coop to roost.

I clearly remember one afternoon when we stood by the truck and watched what appeared to be small puffs of smoke rising from the ground ahead of us. 'What do you think?' my father asked, 'Could it be blacks?' We knew little of them and it was one of the frightening thoughts that was not voiced much. We had heard stories in Queensland that the blacks in the Territory were still wild, tribal people. What should we do? We had enough water to avoid the water hole if necessary, so we drove on. When we came closer, our growing tension was released with delighted laughter. What we had seen were hundreds of budge-rigars swooping for water at a billabong — there were so many of them that they had created a black cloud from a distance.

Sometimes we would reach a water hole which, in the heat of the day, made a shimmering mirage that danced and rippled over the dry ground. (If there were dead stock in the water, and this is never a pretty sight, we tried not to notice.) Mum would boil the water in the billy and top up the supply. If it were possible we kids would have a bogey (that was our slang term for a swim) and Mum did a bit of washing.

We could watch the willy-willies coming and going for miles across the plains. Most of them covered a large area and rose into the air, a furious tunnel of dust as far up as you could see, carrying with it branches, tins, sheets of iron, anything in its path. Mum told us that when she saw her first willy-

willy she was told to run out and throw a bucket of water at it. This, they said, would stop it! The joke was on her, she got the lot! I have never tried that, but to this day I still stand and point a finger at a willy-willy — this is supposed to turn them away. I'm sure it works. Old habits die hard.

The stations along the way were very good to us, and gave us fresh meat as well as salted corned beef, and there were always a few loaves of bread for us children. The women always offered Mum a cup of tea, and it was a real treat for her to have another woman to talk to. If there were children there they would be as shy as we were, and by the time we got around to talking to each other, it was time to hit the road again.

About halfway across the Barkly we picked up a chap humping his bluey. We rarely passed another vehicle, and we were amazed when we saw the figure of a man on foot in the distance. He told us he was walking the stock route, looking for work. All he had in the way of tucker was tea, sugar and rice. He said a little rice went a long way, and it kept well. While he was with us, Mum insisted he share our meals, and he seemed grateful. We gave him a lift to Newcastle Waters, and after leaving there we never saw or heard of him again.

•

Newcastle Waters Cattle Station, was a crossroads and, as well as the usual station buildings, boasted a police station and store-cum-post office. We had reached the centre point of our journey. We stayed overnight, restocked our supplies, and then headed north, following the dirt track along the telegraph line which linked Alice Springs with Darwin.

We had no mishaps on the way. The next stop was at Daly Waters Station, where there was a store; then Maranboy where a mine operated. Only one family was living there — the manager with his wife and two teenage daughters. While our mothers talked, the girls and I shyly eyed each other, full of curiosity, listening to every word of our parents' conversations, never really having one of our own.

At Maranboy, Dad talked to the men about the prospect of work and they told him the railways were employing men. So we went the last fifty miles into Katherine, reassured. Katherine was a small town built on the river, and we all liked the place immediately. We set up camp on the river bank, which was beautiful. Even in the hottest part of the day, you could find a spot on the steep, sloping sides to sit and cool off, or take a bogey in the river. The wide main street had a dirt road, and a scatter of shops and one hotel, down one side. The railway was on the other. The Katherine Hotel was owned by Tim O'Shea and, as this was the traditional meeting place in any out-back town, we headed there to find out all we could about the place, and the district.

The O'Sheas had six lovely daughters, and Tim himself was a legend. He was feared and respected and, I believe, kept law and order pretty much himself. Mrs O'Shea was a lovely lady. She asked Mum in for a cup of tea, and gave us some biscuits.

With Dad's experience in Queensland, it wasn't hard for him to get work with the Northern Territory railways. We stayed in Katherine while he registered for work, then headed south again to Maranboy, which was between Katherine and Mataranka, where he had been assigned. He was in charge of the lifting gang. After the plate-layers and dog men had finished their part, hammering in the large metal spikes that fixed the metal railway lines firmly to the wooden sleepers, Dad's gang levelled the lines. They packed and lifted the lines with his home-made level and they did a marvellous and exacting job.

In those days you arrived at the job site and you were on your own. We pitched tents, moving camp when necessary, as the men worked along the line.

Mum, who was an expert at clearing the 'floor', and watering it down to lay the dust, prepared the site. For a more permanent camp, we crushed up the red dirt from the antbeds and wet it down to reset into a floor as hard as mud bricks; sometimes we nailed bags over the ground.

We had left our planks and bits of tin behind at Mt Isa, so we had to set about gathering enough materials to set up our bush-timber tables and benches. Dad and the boys went out and chopped down a few suitable trees, and Ethel and I helped Mum set out the cooking fire, and spread out the hessian and tents. After our minimal camps during the trip, it felt quite luxurious to have such things as beds raised up off the ground. Dad chopped the fork of a tree, to form the two wishbones, set them upright in the ground and placed a sapling along each side, to form a bed frame. Mum and I sewed two sugar bags together, stretched them over each bunk, and this made a comfortable bed which offered safety from the snakes (death adders were common there), and anything else that might creep around in the night.

As we were completely isolated at Maranboy, there was no question of any of us going to school. Ted and George were able to get jobs with Dad on the railway construction. Ted was now eleven-and-a-half, George was twenty-one. I helped Mum in the camp and after doing the jobs she had set me, I was free to go off daydreaming and to roam the surrounding bush.

Our family camp was a little way off from the tents of the other men working on the gang, as Mum was the only woman and we were the only children there. A man with a truck came around once a week with food supplies, a sort of travelling shop, or hawker. We got our basic things from him: spuds, onions, sugar, tea, flour, tobacco, tinned milk, syrup, jam, fruit. If we needed anything from 'south', it took three months. The order went into Katherine, then up to Darwin by train. The goods were shipped from Brisbane or Sydney to Darwin, then came down on the train from Darwin and eventually we would receive a battered parcel from the truck at Maranboy.

The stations had to get large quantities of supplies in during the dry time of year, for as soon as the wet season set in most of the roads were closed. We too learned to make our orders carefully, so we would have plenty on hand during the wet.

When we first went out to camp at Maranboy, the mine manager's wife — whom we had met on the way up to Katherine — asked me over to stay the night with her daughters. It was quite an experience for me. I felt they looked down their noses at my old well-washed nightdress, toothbrush and comb. And when we sat down at the starched white tablecloths and dinner napkins, beginning the meal with Grace, I just froze up with shyness and embarrassment. I couldn't get home quickly enough. They probably thought I was a bit primitive, because they never invited me again.

Most of Dad's gang were Greek, and they spoke little English. We thought some of their habits were quite funny. They would put out breadcrumbs and blast away with a shotgun to have fresh poultry. (Two doves, or any other bird, to one pot of spaghetti, they explained to Dad.) They called the crow the ha-ha pigeon, but to us the idea of eating a carrion bird was just terrible!

Sometimes, the blacks would visit our camp. They would stand back, dressed only in loincloths or nagas, holding long spears, and demand, 'Tea, sugar, and baccy'. We were scared at first. Mum would roll a cooked damper across to them, and tell them to go. She was always armed with the shotgun, and we kids hid behind her.

After the job at Maranboy was completed, we were sent to another site, at Birdum with the same Greek gang.

•

EVEN AT THIRTEEN years of age, I still longed for a doll (I have never had a real doll). I could drive the truck, was a good shot with a rifle, and generally a fairly capable sort of girl, but always a bit of a dreamer. One of the mail order catalogues said, 'Fill in this coupon and we will send you thirty shillings worth of flower seeds. When you have sold them, and sent in your money, we will send you a celluloid doll.' I sent for the seeds, it didn't dawn on me that there would be no one to sell them to. Mum was the only woman in the camp and there was no such thing as a garden at Maranboy. Seeds such as poppies, sweet peas and stocks were not for the Territory climate. I was stuck with them!

I can't remember what my mother thought of the whole deal, but when the company wrote asking for their money, she paid it, and I got my coveted doll. She was beautiful. I called her Maud, which was my mother's middle name. Her head and arms all moved, she had no hair, and was stark naked. I found an old hankie and made a nappie for her, and then set about getting something for her to wear! Ethel was just as thrilled with her as I was, so I let her play with her too. Although I was getting a bit too old for dolls, there were times I could have cut Ethel's legs off at the shoulders when she would rearrange Maud, or take her off to play!

We still had the gramophone, which I loved. I would play it and sing and dream that one day I would be a star. I also sent stories and letters and poetry to the *North Queensland Register*. This was a weekly newspaper which covered news, sport, and particular news from the outback, and it published letters from readers. My grandfather had written in regularly, years earlier, under the pen-name of 'Bronco'. It was the only newspaper for bush people, and for many was their sole source of information about the outside world. I wrote to the 'Children's Corner', and because I was from so far away, my letters must have had news the other kids liked to read. I became a favourite and was regularly published.

Once I became interested in writing, Ethel and Maud were left to their own devices. I received letters from many other children wanting to become friends with me, and replied to nearly all of them. My mother said that I had a hundred penfriends; but I enjoyed it. Perhaps, one day, I would be a writer. Mum was a good listener, and she enjoyed listening to my stories, and reading the letters I received — we both looked forward to mail day.

One of my penfriends was another girl named Maisie, and we wrote to each other for years until finally, after marrying, we lost touch with each other. Then in 1986 she saw a documentary film, *Frontier Women*, in which I appeared, and she wrote to me again. After some fifty years, we have resumed our correspondence and friendship.

One of Dad's men had been a schoolteacher. He lent me books to read, and would explain them to me. He taught me a lot. The two lessons which have always stood me in good stead were: 'Never lose your temper, if things aren't going right, just walk away,' and 'Never say things you might be sorry for.' Although I wasn't always able to apply this advice, I used to think he was a wise old gentleman. Mr Rowe also gave me books to read, like Tolstoy's *Essays*. They were right over my head, but a chapter a day was the order, then in the evening, he would try to explain. Tolstoy's world was all so strange to me and I must admit I never really understood the readings. But though he might have thought me thick as a brick when I couldn't comprehend the complex plots set in foreign scenes, we both enjoyed our talks.

We also had a Greek chap teaching Ted his language. He could say the alphabet and could speak a few words. I only learned to say, 'The train is coming in tomorrow morning' — which has never been of any use to me, it's not the sort of thing you can throw into a conversation — and a few Greek swear words which were handy if Mum was within earshot!

Mum loved music, but played only by ear; she made a steel guitar. It was a kerosene tin with a square piece cut out on one side. A piece of pine wood about two inches wide and eighteen inches long was attached to this; nails held the steel strings at both ends. She tuned it as best she could to the old 'My Dog Has Fleas' and used a piece of nail for the plectrum. We had great fun with this old guitar, singing along with her. One of the men in the camp made us a little jointed man with a stick fitted into his back, and if you held him and moved the stick up and down to music, he would tap dance, to our great delight.

Mum also played an accordion, the mouth organ, jew's harp, the musical saw, and blew a pretty mean gum leaf. We kids would join in with a comb and paper — simple as it sounds, it made an eerie and rather haunting sound. I had a banjo, which I had learned to play by ear. My first effort was 'The Wearing of the Green'. It must have been very repetitious because my practising nearly drove Dad crazy — 'Pluck, pluck, pluck,' he said. 'Go into the scrub and practise will you!' I did, but never at any stage did I dream of becoming a great musician!

We never really mixed socially with the single men in the camp, and had very few visitors, so our musical evenings were usually just among ourselves.

•

We lived in the Maranboy-Birdum district for nearly two years. It was peaceful, untouched country. I spent hours lying in the grass watching the beautiful formations of clouds during the October and November build-up to the wet; then when it came, we loved playing in the rain. We didn't miss the company of other children. Our life was filled with the bush, which was our entertainment and our teacher.

Ethel was seven years younger than I, and spent

most of her time around Mum. My brother Jim and I often used to shoot at targets — I never had the stomach for killing living things. Jim was a bit of a show-off and reckoned he could shoot the eye out of a pigeon at a hundred yards and that *I* couldn't hit the dunny if I was locked in it! That sort of comment always made me determined to prove him wrong, and ensured some hot competition.

My father had only the most basic needs, and very few wants. He could neither read nor write. I think his favourite pastime was fishing. From Mataranka we would go to a group of billabongs called the Warlock Ponds, where we would sit for hours with a fishing line in our hands. Very rarely did we catch any fish. The barracuda, a lung fish and full of bones, was unpalatable; but the little bream was sweet. Nothing is as peaceful as sitting on the bank of a creek with a fishing line in your hand with the birds and bush noises, little horse-flies landing on reeds along the water's edge and native bees hopping from one water-lily to the next. Perhaps you have a little snooze in the warm sunshine.

Out of Mataranka, we saw Maluka's old grave. In this quiet resting place, overgrown with grass, the only sign of life was the thump of a kangaroo or grazing stock. Maluka was an Aboriginal word, meaning old man or old mate, given to Aeneas Gunn, the manager on Elsey Station in 1902. Maluka appears in Jeannie Gunn's book *We Of The Never Never*. The word 'muligga' is still used around Pine Creek, with the same meaning. It seems 'maluka' was the way Jeannie Gunn spelt the same word.

The largest python that I have ever seen was killed in this district: twenty-one feet long. Someone had stretched it across the road. It looked like a long thin sapling. We were always told to stand still if we saw a snake. One went between my legs once and, believe me, it wasn't easy to stand there. The few moments the snake took to slither through felt like hours and after I was safe to run away, I shook all over with delayed fear. One night a python slid over me while I was in bed. It felt like a heavy piece of rope being pulled across me. I just held my breath, and it seemed to take ages to go across; I was too scared to move anyway.

We always had Sunday dinner. This included sweets — tinned fruit, syrup dumplings, or a steamed pudding — cooked in the camp oven. We would bathe and tidy up for it, making it a little change from the routine of the week.

Every evening, Dad would roll his cigarettes for the next day. He did this all his life. Each end of the cigarette was rolled tightly in a twist to keep the moistness in. He filled a tobacco tin with his quota. I could roll them and would often help him. He always took a billy of cold tea to work too, a better thirst-quencher than water!

One of the advantages of living in the bush was the chance to save your money. So once the railway job had been completed after the New Year in 1929, my family was ready to move on. For the adventure of crossing new country and seeing more of Australia, we decided to travel down the centre. Dad was looking on it more as a holiday, rather than looking for work. But the end of the wet was the wrong time to travel, as the only road was a dirt track along the overland telegraph line. It was now saturated and scattered with sticky, bottomless puddles.

Wet season or not, Dad was anxious to make a start, and argued it would only be wet down as far as Newcastle Waters. We children were pleased at the prospect of moving again, and once more the planning and packing up meant an air of excitement about the camp. We were looking forward to a change.

None of us could have foreseen the trouble which lay ahead. If we had, I guess we would not have been so eager to be on our way.

· IV ·

1929: OUR GREAT OVERLAND TREK

BECAUSE THE PROSPECT of our new adventure was so exciting, I decided to keep a diary. I packed a school exercise book and a few good pencils and began writing like a very grown-up reporter on 'The Adventures of Mayse Dowling' the first day:

*We had fixed 26 February 1929 as our date of departure from
  Mataranka, to start our great adventure through the centre
  of Australia.*
*Although we had lived in Maranboy and Mataranka for two
  years, and had learned to suffer the heat, flies and
  mosquitoes, and numerous other Northern Territory pests, we
  felt a little sad at leaving.*
*We were excited as well! What a day, dragging portmanteaus to
  the truck, falling over swags and shaking hands with friends
  all at the same time. And work? Even the laziest of the
  Dowling family toiled like little beavers . . .*

As a complete anti-climax to that day, we found that the train carrying our final order of supplies had been held up until the following day, so we could only go to the railhead, twenty miles away. The wet season was at its peak and we had heavy rain the night before.

As if to prove the wisdom of those who had warned us against trying to make the trip in the wet, we immediately struck trouble with the boggy roads. Some parts were waist-deep in water. It took us most of the day to get to the Number Two Bore at the Birdum River, where we were to camp to await the train.

Dad gave two men a lift as far as the railhead. When we arrived they and my two brothers decided to take their guns into the bush to do a bit of hunting before dark. The Birdum River is dry most of the year, but in the wet it runs strongly and there is abundant game, so they thought they may be able to supplement our tucker box with a bush turkey or two. This is a delicious delicacy, cooked either as a roast or a stew in the camp oven.

I ended my 'Day One' diary entry:

Our first excitement! As darkness began to shroud us and no hunting party came home, Father came to the conclusion that they were lost. He fired three shots in quick succession, into the air — bang, bang, bang.

Then through the still night we heard shots fired in answer. More shots were fired, spotlights flashed and hurricane lamps were lit; we built a big fire and cooee-ed. Then at about 10 o'clock they returned to camp, wet and exhausted from their walk, but with enough wind to try to make us believe that they knew where they were, but didn't know which direction to take to find camp. We believed that!

The first night out was so wet that the Birdum River rose above its banks, soaking the clayey black soil of the road, and we were forced to stay camped there for several days. In my diary I recorded one of the nights we spent there:

4 March 1929. The next night it rained much harder. The tent sagged, my stretcher gave way and after wrapping my little sister up in the rugs, I buried my toes firmly in the mud, and then sat on my haunches against the collapsed bed, resting my head on my sister's bed, and tried to sleep. Water ran in from all quarters, the mosquito net fell down and there wasn't a dry thing left. Ted and Jim found refuge in Father's lorry, but after a while they left it and stood beside Mother's car. Taking off their wet pyjamas, they wrapped themselves in the motor rug and went to sleep curled up on the back seat.

Mum and Dad were so concerned with trying to keep tents up and the stored food and supplies dry, that they entrusted Ethel to me. As I knew they were also wet and exhausted, I did not

No Place for a Woman   38

complain, and tried to get myself comfortable and Ethel back
to sleep. It didn't take her long to go to sleep again with me
nursing her, but the water rushed around my poor bare feet,
and together with what poured through the top of my tent, I
was as wet as a shag. It dripped on my back, my wet hair
gave me a headache, the cold air gave me toothache and I
could not sleep. The lightning and thunder rolled and
flashed all night. I wished I was a fish, a frog, or even a
duck!

When daylight finally came, it took some time to find wood dry
enough to start a fire. Once it got going we clustered around
it like bees to a honeypot. It was on this morning that for the
first time in my life, I fainted. Instead of going out in the
fresh morning, I had to stay in bed. The back seat of the car!

Another evening, while we were still waiting out the
weather, we visited a small blacks' camp, which we
had seen nearby. There were two old men, two
lubras, and three piccaninnies, in a mia-mia with a
couple of dozen skin-and-bone dogs. Dad gave the old
fellows some tobacco and one old man went off to put
on trousers over his loin cloth for the occasion. We sat
and watched them dance and sing until they were
exhausted. Then they told us a bit of their history,
and described corroborees and places they had visited.
We could not speak their language, so we communicated in hesitant pidgin English. On other days they
showed us how to monkey-climb trees, how to throw
spears and a nulla-nulla, or entertained us with singing, dancing and didgeridoo-playing.

A few days later, we had moved no further. The
rain just kept coming down and the river rose up
again each time the road was beginning to look passable. The wait was frustrating us all, but the cheery
atmosphere of our camp hadn't been dampened too
much, which is reflected in the humorous entry in my
diary on 1 March:

We do have company. The frogs are out in full force. The first
night we camped here, one old fellow kept croaking, 'You
can't get through, you'll bog! You can't get through, you'll
bog!' over and over, and it seems he was right!

39   1929: Our Great Overland Trek

A few days later, I wrote:

Tonight we were the guests of Mr George Hunter. Mr Hunter first came to the Northern Territory in the year 1881. His chief occupation has been ganger on the overland telegraph line, which connects Darwin and Adelaide.

He has had many exciting adventures, enough in fact to fill a whole book. Last year he retired. He now lives in a hut here at Number Two Bore and has a host of fowls, horses and goats and a small garden. The flapping of wings and cackle of hens; the ba-as of goats and dogs barking and clustering around my legs, and trying to lick my hands in friendship; kittens clinging to my skirt; the scent of blossoms — such a homely place — for the first time in my life I realised how delightful a farm was, I just loved it.

Mr Hunter has a very lonely time, but he loves the quietness of the bush. A gramophone and heaps of records keep him company. He has been supplying us with goat meat, eggs and milk, and we are very grateful.

Dad asked one of the old blacks if he thought the rain was going to stop. He scratched his head and said, 'Might be him finish up orright?' Then Dad asked, 'Will we get through?' He thought about it for a while, then asked, 'What sort of motor car you bin gottim? Good fella car, or dat one wheelbarra car? Sposim you gottim good fella car, orright. Sposim you gottim wheelbarra motor car, you bin push push alla time!'

On the tenth day of waiting for the rain to stop at the Number Two Bore, I wrote:

Most of the people around us think we have, er, rooms to let, or that we're elevenpence short of a shilling, leaving in this sort of weather; but we are not alone. A very sad and weary party pulled in here the other day after completing a very boggy and difficult trip from Booroloola. They had an old Dodge truck, and were only bogged twenty-two times!

The driver said to Dad, 'If you take it on in this weather, you won't get through; if you do try, you are a plucky lot of fools!'

The next day, after eleven days of waiting, we 'plucky lot of fools', set out once again. It still poured off and on, and we moved when we could and waited it out between storms. We were all getting very tired of the sight of mud, and our rations were low. Some days, we were able to walk faster than the cars could move.

9 March: *About every five yards we drop into a gilgai hole. We jack up the wheels — we all have our bit to do — and gather antbeds to be packed under each wheel to give it a firm bottom and grip. All day long we trudge along the track, making very little progress.*

A few days later we had the rare sight of another party of travellers:

13 March: *We are not the only ones in trouble. We camp on one side of a big blacksoil flat, and on the other side camp another party. One of their trucks is down well and truly. The others gave us some provisions to carry on with, and a small piece of dried corned meat was relished by us all.*

The next morning everyone met together to consider how to help each other. By three o'clock that afternoon we eventually got across. Soon after, we reached Daly Waters Cattle Station and it seemed our struggle with the wet season might be almost over, because the 'knock-'em-down' winds had started — the winds that flatten the grass down, and which are a sign of the approaching dry season.

I reported to my diary on 18 March:

Our rations are even lower. All that the station could oblige us with was a bag of flour. So, to make things last, we made a meal of pigweed (a wild herb grass). It really isn't bad at all, a bit slimy, that's all.

We only went down two bogs today, and our greatest concern was to know how the eighteen-mile plain was. We had been told that it was more a sea than a plain, and that our cars would disappear completely out of sight in the mud. Imagine our relief when we reached it and found that the water had practically dried up. Tonight we camp like Robinson Crusoe, on a lonely island. There is water all around us. We are going to camp here for a day.

When we reached Newcastle Waters we were down to a quarter of a bag of flour, one tin of jam, two tins of camp pie, and one of sardines — not much between seven of us. My sandy blight was worse, and very painful. All four children had it now, and poor Mother was having a hard time of it, keeping us all comforted. At least when we started out again we had the relief of knowing we had topped up our food and fuel supplies.

After we left Newcastle Waters Station, we crossed the Blue Bush River and drove on along the track to Powell Creek Station.

We passed a bush grave today, so lonely out here. The stone said: 'Dearly loved and sadly missed'. It had a lovely marble cross on it. It was today twenty-three years ago that the man was buried, 1906. I placed a bunch of wild flowers on it. It said that death had been caused by exposure. What a sad and terrible ending.

At Helen Springs Station, we met Mrs Bonning and her teenage daughters Elsie and Edith. They entertained us at afternoon tea, while the men fixed a blow-out. It was a treat for Mother and I to have another woman and the girls to talk to. Dad later told us that Mr Bonning said, 'Before the rains came, the country was so bare you couldn't find a bit of grass to pick your teeth with.'

We travelled through drier country, and had to watch our water supply carefully. We went through Banka Banka Station, past the Tennant Creek Telegraph Station (there was no town there then), to Wycliffe Wells, the Devil's Marbles and then south towards the centre's only town, Alice Springs.

The most memorable visit we made in this stage of the journey was to Singleton Station, where we had morning tea with the owners, the Crooks, and their daughters, Doreen and Kathleen. These girls had lived a lonely life on the station for twenty years. Doreen was twenty-six, and Kathleen was twenty-four. They wore stockmen's trousers and shirts, and had worked very hard since their early teens — mustering and branding cattle, breaking-in horses, drawing water by hand from the bores for the stock in the dry season. They told me that the only town they had ever seen was Alice Springs, and that they only had a faint recollection of this. They took a pride in their ability as stockwomen and were happy, as they'd known nothing else. It made my life seem a very easy one by comparison.

Doreen was to be married just a week after our visit, to a fellow from Tennant Creek Cattle Station. We heard that they went to Adelaide to be married, and returned after their honeymoon to live on Tennant Creek. I often wondered what Doreen thought of her first experience of a city, and how her sister felt having to stay behind.

It had taken us just over a month to reach Alice Springs:

29 March 1929: *This morning we reached Ryan's Well, and Glenmaggie Station, where the manager Mr Nicker, and his daughter Margaret invited us in for morning tea. Just after we pulled in, there was a telephone call from Tea Tree Wells asking if we had arrived safely. This happens all through Central Australia, and it gives us a great sense of security. It's good to know that people care about you.*

Forty miles south of Glenmaggie Station we started to cross the forty-mile Burt Plain, covered in mulga scrub, saltbush, kangaroo and turkey bush, Mitchell grass and other shrubs. After the recent rains, there were masses of wildflowers through it all — they were a glorious sight. The desert seemed to have become one big garden.

Ten miles from Alice Springs we began to climb the MacDonnell Ranges. With their deep red colours, they were spectacular and beautiful in contrast to all the flat country we had covered and I got a stiff neck trying to see everything.

Nearing 'The Alice', we crossed the Todd River, with many camps of Blacks along its banks, and entered the delightful little township. It had just one hotel, a few grocery stores — the main one was owned by Wallis Fogarty — and a baker who, we were told, rose to the occasion only when orders came in, as most of the population made their own bread. There was an Australian Inland Mission base at The Garden — one of the oldest homes in Alice Springs — and a police station and a school. There was also a tennis court, and a racecourse, and Chinese vegetable gardens along the banks of the Todd, which supplied the town with fresh produce.

The night we arrived, there was to be a send-off for the schoolmistress, Mrs Stanley. She had taught there for sixteen years: white children in the mornings, and half-caste children in the afternoons.

Next Monday there is going to be a race meeting. Six horses with two in each race! Punt for a place and you can't lose! At the race ball on the Monday night, the dance floor is made out in the open, with a square of canvas pegged tight over it.

2 April 1929: We leave this little town of Alice Springs with its lovely weeping pepper trees. We enjoyed our stay, even if a lot of the time was spent mending punctures. It was so cold while we were here that the water froze in the pipes overnight, and buckets of water left out were solid ice in the morning. About a mile out of town we crossed the Todd River again and went through Heavitree Gap, which, we are told, is where the railway line will pass.

4 April, 1929: Out of the Macdonnell Ranges, and fifteen miles on we came to the head of the railway construction works, and the beginning of the notorious Depot Sandhills. These sandhills really are sandhills! There must be millions of them. All the fine powder-like red sand is banked along shrubs and spinifex clumps, forming waves with hundreds of ripples on their surfaces; and here and there is a lonely desert oak throwing some welcome shade — these trees make an eerie wailing sound when the wind blows through them.

Here began the most dangerous part of our trip, because the road was no longer visible. Every traveller had to cut out their own track and shortly after they had passed, the winds swept all sign of it away again. Most people going this way carry rolls of matting, which they throw down in the wheel tracks. We did not have any, so we did it the hard way — all hands pulling up spinifex to lay in front of the tyres.

One of the men at a railway camp told Dad this story:

One swagman heading to Alice met up with another who had just come from there, and they camped together. Next morning, after a conference, the two decided to travel together and go back toward Alice. After trudging for six hours, the one from the south said to the one who'd come through from Alice the day before: 'Where are those Depot Sandhills you've been telling me about?'
'Well' said the other, very puzzled, 'I'm hanged if I know, they were here yesterday!'

We travelled in a southerly direction over what seemed like a moving sea of sandhills, our only guides the overland telegraph line and the few government bores — each of which was marked by a large above-ground tank to hold the water — and now and again a river. One almost dry river meandered through the sandhills so much, that we had to cross it several times.

Then we came to Horseshoe Bend. Our vehicles were poised on the top of a small hill, ready to wind down the rocky hills through a beautiful pass. It was a sight to behold — like a small oasis, the river gums made a rim of green along the creek which wound around the base of a small gorge in the shape of a horseshoe. At the bottom of the descent lay rich red sand and patches of gibber stones, dotted with areas of green grass that had sprung up after the rains. We stopped and enjoyed it as a camping site, before heading out again into the desolate landscape of the surrounding desert.

My diary entry reads:

Here in the midst of such beauty is the tiny town of Horseshoe

Bend. It has a hotel, general store, telegraph station and a benzene dump. Population: about ten people.

8 April 1929: It is quite a sight to see strings of camels tied to one another, harnessed and packed, generally driven by blackfellows. It is funny to see them riding a camel, for having no saddle they have to sit behind the hump, practically on the tail. Yesterday I saw two blacks riding camels and shepherding sheep.

9 April 1929: There are many lonely graves along the track. One we passed this morning had a beautiful marble headstone. It had been there since 1883. We were told that we would pass two graves close together along the road, those of a father and son. It had happened that they ran out of water while travelling this way. The son sat his father under a shady bush, and took a billy can and went back to find a well. When he reached the well, the only thing he could find to lower the billy was a piece of string. He carefully drew up the full billy with its precious water; but while it was too far away for the boy to grab, the string broke. The son was found dead by the well, and his father where he had left him waiting, waiting, waiting...

•

AFTER CROSSING the border into South Australia, we travelled over sand and gibber country. No grass or trees could be seen for miles; the heat threw mirages ahead of us and the glare and wind were almost unbearable.

10 April 1929: The sandstorm raged all night. When I awoke this morning I was lovely and warm, and the cover on top of me felt rather heavy. It was a tough job getting my head out, and when I did, Heavens, I couldn't believe my eyes! I was practically covered in sand.

We travelled day after day through more sandhill country, getting bogged nearly as many times as we had in the wet mud at the outset of our journey. We were now in very dry country and water was scarce:

12 April 1929: The only water we have is salty, and very little of that. We have in the past drunk all sorts of water. Here, if we strike trouble, we can survive on parakeelya. This is a *form of succulent herb which grows in the desert, and which has green leaves similar to pigweed. They are ninety per cent water which is very salty, but it is food and drink. The stock love it. We've been told that stock coming from places like this have to be taught to drink proper water!*

That day we pulled into Mt Eba Sheep Station, where we got about three pounds of mutton. It was the first fresh meat we'd had since Alice Springs — so our meal that night was like a feast.

We often saw dingoes. One evening we saw two white ones at the side of the road — a most unusual sight — but they ran off before we could get a good look at them. Not long after this, our dog, Rover, had a fit. He must have taken a dingo bait. Dad slit his ears to make them bleed — this was supposed to help get some of the poison out of his system — and we poured salty water down his throat to make him sick, but his hind legs cramped, and he had convulsion after convulsion. We could do nothing but rub him down. In tears, I tended him. He was a wonderful pet and had been everywhere with us for seven years. We thought we'd lost him, when suddenly he began to show signs of pulling through — our remedies had worked.

16 April 1929: Not far from Coondamby Station, we looked down into a deep basin among the hills, with a big salt lake at the bottom. Here, our radiator on the truck went dry and nearly caused a fire. We had just started up again when bang! Another puncture, so tonight we camp at a well on a treeless tableland on a bed of stones.

We know where we came from, but we honestly don't know where we are going. We get information from station owners about the nearest and best 'cut-across' route to the Western Australian road. No one knows definitely, so we have decided to go to Port Augusta and take the longest and safest route. There is nothing around us but stones and treeless plains. It hasn't rained here for seven years.

At the Lake Windabout railway cottages we met two men who had been travelling north in a Ford truck that had broken down. Dad went through all the information they had on the track ahead. After hearing how meat-hungry we were, one of the men said, 'Oh, we never go short of meat. We have plenty on hand, you can have some!' 'Where did you get it?', asked Dad, because the sheep stations we had passed through had told us they didn't even have enough mutton to feed themselves — they were living off tinned meat, while their sheep died in their thousands, as those that were left were just skin and bone. 'Why, over at the well, they come in every evening', he said. 'Emu!' We accepted the dark oily meat, and Mum cooked it. Those who ate it enjoyed it, but I just didn't have the stomach for it.

We stayed four days in Port Augusta. George left us to return to Queensland. Dad put our two vehicles into the garage for a going-over and we stocked up on provisions. Ted always went with Dad in the truck, and had helped him drive ever since we had set out from Mataranka. In Port Augusta a policeman pulled him over because he was an under-age driver: twelve years old. He wanted to know why Ted wasn't in school. When he heard our story and how Ted had already worked over a year driving the truck before we set out, he let us off.

We set out with renewed vigour to cross the Nullarbor Plain to Western Australia. The road followed the coastline in its first stages, and occasionally we would look out and glimpse the sea. We were able to buy fresh fish and oysters, which made a very welcome change to our diet. As we went west we also had the novelty of driving on roads bordered by two parallel fences. We had never seen fences or cultivated wheat like this before.

We were surprised to find that the hospitality of these farmers was not like those of the station people in the Northern Territory. They made it quite clear that they did not welcome travellers to call in, so we camped away from the homesteads, usually near a bore or tank. Once in the Nullarbor country, we found ourselves in more familiar desert, often driving over big salt pans. We came to gold-mining camps, and then to the town of Coolgardie.

30 April 1929: Looking at Coolgardie one would think it was a ruin left after a war. The streets are deserted and only a few stores are kept open. Great stone buildings have fallen down and others are just crumbling away. Drooping pepper trees seem to weep for the utter ruin and desolation. They said Coolgardie at its peak had a population of 17 000 — and now it's practically deserted.

I enjoyed this part of the journey. I loved the wild-flowers, especially the beautiful Sturt's Desert Pea which covered the plains in a carpet of green, scarlet and black. I also studied the water tanks for the messages and bits of poetry that other travellers had scratched on them, often adding a poem or note of my own.

After the long stretch across the Nullarbor we started to come into wheat-growing country again and small towns became more frequent. Soon the towns seemed so close together that we joked that it was like one long street running into Perth.

We reached Perth on 7 May 1929, and stayed for two months. We camped in a paddock near a farm on the outskirts of the city. Dad had had the idea that he would find work or possibly go into a business venture. He became friendly with the farmer, who took him around the district and tried to talk him into taking up land. Luckily for us all — for Dad had no experience of farming — he decided against it. He said he couldn't understand how anyone could succeed and reckoned he'd counted fifty-three species of poisonous bushes which kill stock, while looking at places for sale.

We loved to walk around Perth, exploring the beautiful parks along the river and looking at all the wonderful things the shop windows offered. It was my first big city and I had reason to believe it was probably Mum's too. We were a couple of country bumpkins, and must have given some sales ladies a field day. Mum got talked into buying a black-and-white checked skirt, with the checks about two inches square; it was a skirt she didn't like and never wore. I reckon they could have sold us the Swan River if they'd set their minds to it!

One day Ted, who by now was getting to be quite a good mechanic and who was very keen on aviation, had a flight over the city in one of the big three-engined Hercules planes. They took passengers up for half-hour spins at two guineas. He was so excited and thrilled he talked about it for days.

•

Although it was mid-winter, cold and often wet in Perth, we enjoyed our two months there, and all of us felt very reluctant to get moving again. We set out up the West Australian coast in mid-July and once we were on the road again, and the new sights aroused our interest, we soon swung into our travelling routine.

19 July 1929: *Our first stopover for a rest was at Meekatharra. We are still feeling the cold, mostly because of the wind. It seems to chill you to the bone. Each time we make camp, Father makes a windbreak around where we sleep to keep out the cold, and we put big stones into the fire to heat up, then wrap them in a towel or bag and put them at our feet. They are as good as hot water bottles. Once you are settled in and your body heats the bed, you can have a good night's rest.*

Meekatharra was a bleak little mining town. Dad tried to get work there, but there was none available, so we moved on.

It's my birthday today, I am sixteen, and for my present my family gave me a joyride in an aeroplane! Gosh, it was lovely. Ever since Ted went on his flight in Perth, I have been dying to

*find out if it was as wonderful as he claimed. My plane was
a little single-seater owned by a Perth millionaire and piloted
by Charles Nesbitt. I wasn't scared. When I tried to wave to
the family on the ground, the wind nearly took my arm off!
Everything looked so small from up there; the railway lines
and trains resembled toys. You felt as if you weren't moving
at all, the plane seemed to be anchored in mid-air, rising and
falling like a row boat. I hated the thought of coming down
again, but rushing towards earth was much more thrilling
than leaving it!*

After a long journey northwards, we were very
excited to reach Broome, as we had heard so much
about the exotic pearling industry.

The town was a scatter of houses, a street of
shops, and hotels, with an ornate Chinatown section
which served the most wonderful and refreshing
lemon squashes we had ever tasted. Most of the
townspeople looked prosperous, and the white men
wore white duck suits, and white linen shoes, with
panama hats or pith helmets. I even saw one man
wearing a monocle and using a cane — like a character
out of some tropical adventure story.

The jetty was the focus of the town — and it
looked high and dry when the tide dropped over forty
feet each day. The divers for the pearling fleets were
mostly islanders. We were told that their diving gear
was very dangerous, as they didn't have proper diving
suits. Some wore lead boots and had their air supply
pumped down to them through hoses. Walking along
the wharf, we saw bits and pieces of this apparatus,
and wondered how men could work under the sea
with such unwieldy equipment.

*8 August 1929: Today we passed a trooper with a string of
Aboriginal prisoners, chained together, working on the road.
It turned my stomach to think this sort of thing still happens.*

The poinciana trees had finished their blooming season and now stood bare of leaves, with big black heavy
seed pods, but the beach, covered with coral and

pretty shells was like an exotic garden for us to explore.

By the second week of August, Dad decided to go into the sandalwood business, and we set out to make camp about fifty miles out from Broome. He had contracted to get twenty-five pounds per ton. The wood, from the quandong trees, had to be stripped of all bark; it was very tedious and hard work. Dad had employed nine Aboriginal helpers.

I am learning things from them. They are more used to whites than those in the Northern Territory. We go bush walking, and they show me how to dig nardoo and grind them into a type of flour. They also point out the trees that store water, and how to tap them; what roots and berries to eat. When they get kangaroo, they light a big fire, and when it burns down, they scoop a hollow in the coals, tuck the tail between the back legs, and the head between the front legs, and drop it in (that dreadful smell of burning fur!), then cover the carcass with the rest of the coal, leaving it several hours to cook. When they take it up from the fire, it looks black and ugly and very unappetising; but when the outer skin is peeled off the flesh looks white and moist, and they always enjoy a feast.

Dad's venture was not a success. After four weeks of labour we had only gathered two and a half tons of wood. We all agreed it was not worth it. So, on 24 September, we folded our tents once again and loaded up to move on. We said farewell to our helpers and they seemed sorry to see us leave.

We headed across the Kimberley towards the Northern Territory. The further out we got from Broome the worse the road became, and we could see the purple skies overhead announcing the beginning of the wet again. We resumed our pattern of camping at bores and tanks and calling at station homesteads for directions and supplies. We were often invited in for a meal or tea, and we looked forward to these occasions, which the station people seemed to enjoy as much as we did.

After days of travel on the roughest roads we had encountered, we finally crossed over the Western Australian border, back into the Northern Territory, following the Murrinjii Track — a very lonely drover's route. We had to carry water in drums: six drums to last fifteen stops. We camped one night on the banks of the beautiful big Victoria River, with its pandanus palms and tropical growth along the banks and all had a very welcome bogey.

We went on to Wave Hill Station, one of those owned by Lord Vestey, then to Pigeon Hole Station and Black Springs, where the air was filled with birds: cockatoos, parrots, galahs and crows in their hundreds, circling and screeching.

When we moved on the next day, Dad's truck was running hot, with the radiator boiling enough to burst. We could only go about two miles, then stop to let it cool down. The track was particularly bad, which didn't help. Later in the afternoon we met a truck with two old Northern Territory friends coming the other way and we stopped and had a great chat. We decided to camp together at Paddy's Springs. From there we took it very easy, stopping to repair the truck at the stations we passed, and finally towing it the last twenty miles into Katherine.

On 8 November 1929, I made my last diary entry of the journey:

We were so pleased to reach Katherine after the rough trip we'd had, the dangers which lurked in so many places and the fears felt so many times. Now help is here, Mother and Father must be so relieved.

Although I didn't say it, I was more than a little relieved myself!

· V ·

1929–1931: NEW PUBLICANS AT PINE CREEK

GETTING BACK TO Katherine again was, in a way, like going home. We had been halfway around the Australian continent during 1929, and this was the one place we felt we knew. It was familiar ground.

The O'Shea family welcomed us for a cuppa and a chinwag about our travels. Mr and Mrs O'Shea tut-tutted when my parents said that they were planning to keep travelling back to Queensland. Then they suggested that we buy the Pine Creek Hotel. 'It's on the market and going cheap,' they said, 'and it would be ideal for you!'

This decision must have taken a lot of thought and soul-searching from the Dowling side, and a lot of prodding and Irish persuasion of the 'Of course you can do it' variety from the O'Shea side. However, as well as their enthusiasm, the O'Sheas had plenty of experienced advice to offer my parents.

Mum and Dad talked the idea over for some time, while we camped on the outskirts of Katherine. There were several factors influencing them. We had been on the road for nearly twelve months already and it had been hard going; we had no immediate work to go to in Queensland; and Dad said that the car and truck were both mechanically pretty sick. This all helped the Pine Creek project sound very attractive. Our finances were sound, so with a deposit and a loan from the bank, we became publicans in Pine Creek overnight: Mum with her limited education, Dad with none and four bush-trained kids!

We purchased the hotel from an outback identity, May Brown. It was described as 'a single-storey building of wood and iron constructed in the old-fashioned way. There are eight bedrooms and accommodation can be made for thirty, with the aid of stretchers on the veranda.'

We packed up our camp gear for the last time, and travelled the sixty-four miles north from Katherine to Pine Creek. We children were excited and anxious to see the place which was to become home. We had heard stories that our grandmother had lived in Pine Creek for a while during the early 1900s, but none of us had ever been there.

It was a small town, sitting between hills which, we were told, were rich in gold. We could see the signs of mine workings here and there. Pine Creek had its boom time in the 1870s, when gold was first discovered. In those days it had attracted a large population of miners, many of whom were Chinese, but when the alluvial gold from the creeks was no longer easily obtained a decade later, the population began to drift away.

As we drove in, we could see the town had dwindled into just a scatter of buildings along the dusty main street which ran parallel to the railway line. There was a general store, a school, a police station, railway station, an Anglican Church and a small town hall. A large old corrugated-iron building was the abandoned hospital. There were a few houses; some were unoccupied, and falling into disrepair. There were vacant lots where others had once been, now covered with the head-high cane grass of the wet season.

The hotel, now the only one in town, was a comfortable-looking old place, built in the typical, rambling, Australian-outback style of timber and galvanised iron, with a cement floor. It was unlined inside, and had wide verandas all the way around it, with large push-out lattice shutters which could be closed to make extra rooms.

It was surrounded by lovely frangipani, poinciana, banana and paw paw trees and patches of lawn, and was partly covered in creepers: Japanese jasmine and mountain rose (commonly named Barmaid's Blush). It had an atmosphere of hospitality and bush comfort, a haven of shade and cool refreshments; it was in fact a place where good humour and relaxed company could be found to relieve the isolation and heat of the outback.

I was sixteen and after living in a tent all my life, it seemed like a palace. We were all delighted with it, and we children wandered around in amazement, exploring all the rooms and becoming adjusted to the fact that we now had such luxuries as real beds, rather than camp stretchers. Mum had a stove to cook on, instead of billy cans and camp ovens! And we thought we were truly civilised.

This really was a completely new life for all of us. We had been taught to look the other way when we passed hotels. It was hard to imagine our family actually living in one.

I could only remember one instance, back in Queensland, when Dad came home after having one too many. Until then, we never thought he drank! He was put to bed — where he raved a bit, saying a few bad words (we didn't think he swore either). Mum put a pillow over his head, and shooed us off outside to play!

•

We were all so happy with the Pine Creek Hotel, we settled into our new lifestyle very quickly. With no experience at all in running a hotel, Mum and Dad were lucky because Mrs McNiece, a very competent woman who had worked for May Brown, agreed to stay on with us. With her assistance, Mum organised the routines, set out tasks for each of us and learnt to manage the business side of the hotel.

My brother Ted and I were expected to work alongside our parents. At fourteen and sixteen we were considered old enough to be part of the family business and do a full day's work. The two younger children, Jim and Ethel went to school.

Dad became a reasonable barman, though Mum always kept her eye on him. (She was known to mark the spirits bottle at the level of the drink inside after the bar closed, to make sure he wasn't sneaking back for a quickie.) Dad, of course, wasn't all that green. He had a bottle of gin hidden in the stables. Mum used to worry when he had to slip off to the toilet so often through the day. She felt he must have had a weak something or other.

The hotel felt very large and spacious to us. Parts of the veranda had been sectioned-off to form an office and our family bedrooms. A passage ran through the centre of the building, and on one side was the bar and billiards room and on the other the dining room, bedrooms and a shower room, and at the back the large kitchen, which became our family gathering place.

On the veranda next to the dining room was the 'Coffee Room'. This was our first-class dining room, where for the privilege of sitting down to white starched serviettes (the tables in both rooms had white tablecloths), and away from the roughnecks in the dining room, you paid an extra sixpence for your meal. Full price of the meal was two shillings and sixpence; dinner, bed and breakfast together cost six shillings.

Both the Coffee room and dining room were fitted out with punkahs (hand-worked fans). These were made up of material pleated and tacked along lengths of board, hung from the ceiling on swivels. They were worked from outside the window by someone pulling on the lengths of rope attached to the punkah. For pocket money, one of the local boys would do this for the hour or so that guests sat in the dining room. It created a beautiful cool breeze, which in the tropics was pure luxury.

A large round container, sitting in a tray of water, was our carbide-gas lighting plant. The carbide was put in the container, and the gas produced by mixing it with water was piped into the hotel and the jets, which when turned on and lit, provided gaslight. We also used kerosene lamps.

Careful not to waste any resource, the powdered residue from the carbide, mixed with water, made a great whitewash, which we used to paint out-houses and wooden fence posts, and to brighten up the kitchen every now and then.

Along one side of the hotel we had another building which provided eight guest rooms. These were lit by candles in holders. Each was furnished with a wooden towel rack, iron bed, and pine dressing-table with washbasin and jug of water. A mosquito net hung from a ring in the ceiling; the bed legs stood in tins of water or oil, to keep the Singapore ants out. My brothers discovered a very sadistic prank to play. They would put a bit of food in the bed and hang a thread of string or cotton down to the floor for the ants to climb. These ants were small, brown, and had a mighty powerful sting.

On the back veranda we had our washing facilities, which seemed very sophisticated to me after our routine of boiling clothes over the camp fires to get them clean. We now had flat irons on the stove, and others which contained red-hot coals; there was a big mangle where one person turned the handle like crazy, while another fed the sheets and pillow slips into the rollers.

Mother had help in the kitchen and a big fuel stove, which was a great luxury — even if it meant constantly stoking a fire in tropical conditions. It was a far cry from the camp cooking she had done for so many years.

We baked most of our own bread, but ordered some by train from Katherine or Darwin. This made a welcome change from making the bread ourselves when we had a lot of guests at the hotel. It did not worry us if the bread was a couple of days old by the time we got it. A sprinkle of water, and a few minutes in the oven, and it was as good as fresh — almost! One Katherine baker, named Crook, had a large sign outside his corrugated-iron shop which read 'Crook Bread and Buns'. He was a bit of a character and used to say 'Come in and have one of my crook buns!'

Our butcher, George Stevens, was one of the local cattlemen. Since we had no refrigeration, he had to deliver fresh meat often and we used a lot of corned meat. Cool storage consisted of Coolgardie safes. They were big flywire containers which were kept cool by flannel strips hanging down the sides and dampened by water trays, top and bottom.

The Chinese men from the Pine Creek 'Chinatown' grew vegies in season that suited our climate — pumpkins, cucumbers, tomatoes, Chinese cabbage, snake beans, bananas, paw paws.

By 1928, only a small group of Chinese lived in Pine Creek. The Chinese had been the first people of ethnic origin to settle as a group in the Northern Territory. They were brought in from Singapore in 1874, to work as labourers in the mines. Later, groups came from elsewhere in Asia, but those in Pine Creek came from South China. At one time the Chinese community had numbered about four thousand, with a European population of fewer than one thousand. Now, mostly old men remained, who had built themselves huts and formed a sort of shanty town at the back of the Eleanor mine, about a mile from Pine Creek.

There was a story that once the Chinese miners had demanded more money from their bosses. When the demands were refused, they all went down to the blacksmith's and had him take an inch off each of their shovels!

They had a joss house which was adorned with figures, carvings and hung with bright gold and orange cloth. We often went there during our walks. It wasn't unusual to see these old men lying around smoking opium. I believe that as it had been their custom, they were granted permission to have a certain amount for their own use by the government. They were a quiet and friendly people, but kept to themselves.

The small square bottles which contained the opium were made of thick glass, with a small centre. We called them 'tear bottles', as we also believed the Chinese men wept and caught their tears in the bottles and sent them home to their families. The only time we ever saw them in town was when they would come to the hotel, each with their two baskets hanging from bamboo yokes, full of fruit and vegetables which they had grown in their gardens.

I worked under the supervision of my mother and Mrs McNiece. She had worked for a big hotel down south in Melbourne, and she was a hard taskmaster for me. If I did not do a job properly, I had to do it again. So, before long I learned to make beds, set and wait on tables, mangle and iron the washing, sweep and mop, and hose down the bar, even cook. There wasn't much I couldn't do, and I was a pretty good barmaid to boot!

Our customers were from the mines or stations and the few Pine Creek locals: the railway workers, or lizards as they were known — because they ran up and down the tracks repairing them — the policeman, school teacher, station master, and store keeper. In those days, of course, no woman customer would ever enter the bar.

Despite the fact that few of the stations had womenfolk on them, I noticed that the lads were always dressed 'rough, but clean' when they came into the hotel — good, tough, moleskin trousers, strong leather boots, and the old stetson hat, which rarely left the owner's head.

For all their rough exteriors, most of these men were gentlemen and always treated women with consideration and respect. If a swear word slipped out in conversation when we were within earshot, it was followed by an apology. On the other hand, females also respected the bar as the men's private sanctuary, and we knew that we weren't supposed to listen in on their talk.

Of course there were punch-ups every now and then. One determined, bull-headed pair that I remember, fought and fought out on the lawn until they lay exhausted beside each other in the grass. After a while, too tired to fight any more, they adjourned to the bar to recover; getting a second wind, they went out on the flat to continue. In the end, both were bruised and exhausted, and neither had won. I suppose it was one way to fill in the day!

It wasn't long before I became the darling of the hard drinkers. They would complain, 'That bloody old George Dowling wouldn't give us a free heart-starter in the morning.' I felt sorry for these lonely old fellows who had let the drink get the better of them, and I became known as a pretty soft touch, as I would always give in to them. Because some had the shakes so badly, I would have to hold the glass for them as well. It was probably the metho and rubbish that they drank between times that knocked them about.

Most of the time I enjoyed the work. I felt grown-up, helping with the responsibilities of the hotel. There was a sense of satisfaction in it: starching and ironing, out on the veranda overlooking the garden with that lovely fresh clean smell. Flat irons with detachable handles were set on the hot top of the stove to warm, and we had lumps of beeswax ready to iron everything stiff and smooth. We would gossip with each other while we worked, and quite often the local girls and women would call in and talk to us while we finished off a task.

Ted worked with Dad; he drove the truck and carted the wood for the stove and laundry copper. He met the train and collected the beer and stores, so he was as busy as I was. We were always very close, and would enjoy a quiet chat together when we'd finished our work.

All our beer came by sea to Darwin, and then down 156 miles to us by train. It only came in large bottles, each encased in straw outer covering; five-dozen lots were packed in wooden cases. As there was no other way to keep the bottles cool, we would keep them wet and covered with wet bags. The lads would say that if Dad was in a good mood he would throw two buckets of water over the case; if he had a 'dirty liver', he would only throw one!

Only wine, spirits and bottled beer (two shillings a large bottle) and lemon squash, were sold in the bar in those days. There was no such thing as beer on tap, or mixed drinks. Spirits were taken either straight, or with water, and the spirit glasses had a nip line etched into them.

One day a stranger walked into the bar and with a loud clatter, he dumped a sugar bag on the counter. He told Dad that it contained a gun and a knife, and if he didn't give him some grog we'd be sorry. This didn't daunt Dad for a minute. He might have been a slightly-built man, but he had a lot of guts. He just sprang over the counter, and said he was going to hammer the hell out of the bloke. The character lost no time in grabbing his sugar bag and getting out of the place.

It was the law that a light must burn over the front door of the hotel at night to guide the weary traveller — not that we had many of those at that time. In the wet season — November to April — the light guided the flying ants, stink beetles, and lavender bugs to our hotel. The flying ants would hit the light, land, and just shrug off their wings and crawl away. You could literally pick up buckets of wings off the floor.

The hotel was never very crowded, although we had a steady flow of locals, the only really busy times were when the train stayed overnight — which always brought a few extra people.

In a small place like Pine Creek, it didn't take long to get to know the locals. On train nights, we would gather out on the front veranda. It was always a special night for the town, as it brought news and new faces. The mine crews, and sometimes the station people would come in to collect their stores and mail and stay overnight. We would set up the old gramophone, and dance, or just sit out on the grass — the coolest place — and talk. It gave us young ones a chance to get together with our friends and have a giggle — always within sight of our parents, of course!

That lawn out in front of the hotel saw many a story and many a fight over the years! About ten o'clock every evening the 'Doctor' would arrive. This was the evening breeze and was most welcome. Unfortunately, the Singapore ants were also on the prowl for a nice, soft, damp spot — like under the arms, or around the neck or legs. If you saw someone jump up and leave in a hurry, you could bet your boots an ant had found a spot too private to scratch in company!

Most of the mine crews lived out of the town, in pretty rough conditions. The main mine in operation was the Hercules — later renamed the Eureka — then renamed again the Moline. It still exists today.

Many of the mines had their own small crusher, and they treated the ore as best they could. Some of these mines were in such seemingly impossible outposts, it was amazing how they ever got the equipment there, even with horse and bullock wagons. The steam engines and large steel wheels were so heavy and bulky that transport was a mammoth undertaking and not a challenge for the fainthearted.

We did not see the people from the stations very often, but when they did come in they were usually good company. The ringers — stockmen — would have no work on the stations for the three or four months of the wet season; they would set up a bit of a camp somewhere just out of town and come to the hotel for meals, drink, and company; they'd usually have a good time until their savings ran out, when they'd ride back to the stations for another season of cattle work.

Our first taste of tourism came soon after we settled into Pine Creek. Run by an enterprising man named Bertie Bond, this was a real touch of the outside world. The old tour bus would arrive with southern people wearing crazy tropical clothes, the ladies in large check shorts (we weren't sure if they were long shorts or short longs). The best part was the music. Mr Bond had rigged a speaker on the top of his bus and, on a clear evening, we could get music. Wireless reception has never been good in Pine Creek, because of the mineral belt that surrounds it. So, this was a touch of magic.

Sometimes we would hold a burning stump for his party. Today, I suppose you would call it a barbecue. We would light a big fire at the end of a large stump. There were officials appointed, like 'the knight of the burning stump', 'chief hot cinder', and 'the wet blanket'. Everyone brought their own food and drink and sat around swapping yarns. If you were called upon to perform an item, whatever it might be — sing, recite, tell a story — you did your best, then it was your turn to call on someone else. My contribution during these evenings around the burning stump was usually a song. I rather fancied myself as a blues singer — all without musical accompaniment, of course.

Our rule was that however big a fool you made of yourself during the evening, it died with the fire. No chiacking next day.

The fire has been dead on *this* one many years ago, so I'll be forgiven for mentioning that one night a travelling minister — who was a good sport and a good friend — had to be held up while he gave us a very stern lecture on the evils of demon drink, much to the entertainment of the party gathered on the lawn.

Occasionally the buffalo shooters would come in. They lived in camps out near the buffalo herds — mostly in Arnhem Land. There wasn't any rivalry that I remember between the different buffalo catchers. It was a big country, and they had a gentle-men's agreement between them, on who would work an area. Tom Cole was one of the best buffalo shoot-ers that I knew and he would come in on his breaks and spend some time with us. He became a good friend.

From what I heard about buffalo shooting, I never had any desire to see it. It seemed a very cruel way to make a living. The shooters hunted the buffalo on horseback, carrying rifles. When they came across a herd, the riders marked out the animals they wished to kill and pursued them at full gallop either shooting them in the spine, or ham-stringing the back legs in order to bring them down. They would go on chasing the herd marking off more buffalo in this way, until they had as many as they could handle. The animals were left maimed and alive, waiting for the group of skinners to catch up. If they were shot dead, they would rot within hours in the hot climate. The skinners would put the poor beasts out of their misery, skin them, and pile the hides on the back of a pack horse.

•

After all the years of following Dad's work, Pine Creek was my first real home. I realised what it meant to be in a place where you could make permanent friends and live in a community. I can never remember being bored or lonely in Pine Creek and it was a very happy time for all of us.

There were always people around the hotel, but as they were mostly older folk — my parents' age and bar customers — I enjoyed getting out and mixing with the other young people in town. The two Cox families (two brothers had married two sisters, and they lived next door to each other in Pine Creek) had many children between them, and some of the girls were my age. There were also other families, so I had a lively group of friends. We would often pack lunches and go for walks in the bush and have a picnic; sometimes our mothers would take us to Bonrook Station waterhole, or the Copperfield for swims. This is an area to the west of the town, through which runs the Copperfield Creek. It was still functioning as a copper mine then, with a few small diggings still operating.

Later we acquired bikes (mine still a boy's) and we rode around town and over the local hills. In plum season we picked wild plums, later we gathered armfuls of beautiful blue hyacinths. At mushroom time we walked miles for a billyful. When the wild heather was in flower, miles of country would be covered in soft mauve blossoms and we collected bunches of these lovely flowers to take home. We believed that the heather and the rubber shrub seeds were brought to the area in the packing cases brought over by the Chinese migrants. The rubber bush had bunches of leaves and blue and mauve-blue blooms which, when picked, oozed a sticky milky sap. After the flowers came large green pods, which, when mature, burst open to fill the air with silky snow-white wool.

When Mr Finness came to town as head teacher at the school, and brought his family of seven children, it meant great company for me. The eldest girl, Thelma, became my friend. Mrs Finness was a lovely laughing lady, who forever seemed to be washing and ironing. Mr Finness always wore white duck suits to school, and a white pith helmet — which was the formal tropical dress of the time. Everything was starched in those good old days, no wash 'n' wear then — everything except the bras and bloomers, that is! The starch came in little white lumps in a packet. First you mixed it to a paste with cold water and then poured boiling water over it, stirring all the time to make a nice thick glug. If you got to it before your mum added a bit of blue from the blue bag and a few drops of kerosene, it tasted all right! Some of the kids reckoned that with a bit of sugar it was like blanc-mange without milk. Ugh!

We often went riding. The police always had horses which were kept in the paddock, and any of the station jackeroos who happened to be in town with their plant of camp horses, would make a quiet saddle horse available for us to ride. There were plenty of places to go: Bonrook Station, Copperfield, the old police paddock, its high ridges and running water always alive with birds and wild animals, beautiful ferns and millions of leeches. The Chinese gardens had mango trees, banana palms, paw paws, and five corners! When you split open the five corners fruit it had five sections, which formed a star. The old mines, if you were adventurous enough to explore them, were riddled with deep dark tunnels alive with black bats and sleeping snakes.

To some people it may seem like an isolated and boring little outback town to grow up in, but not to us. The whole countryside around us was alive, and full of fascinating things to explore and beautiful places to enjoy.

•

MY FIRST TRIP to Darwin was a very special event, as the Pine Creek cricket team had challenged the Darwin boys to a game. Some of the girls were allowed to go along with them (naturally with a chaperone, damn it!)

Darwin was 156 miles away along a dirt track which followed the telegraph and railway lines: a day's travel and what a rough and dusty day! The back of the truck wasn't the most comfortable place to be, but when you are young — and most of the men were too — it was a giggle a minute for us girls! Some years later the record time by road from Darwin to Pine Creek was broken; the new time was nine hours. We had driven along at about fifteen miles per hour and it took us ten and a half hours! There were no bridges over rivers and creeks and it was particularly slow going around Adelaide River. Today that track is the Sturt Highway.

Darwin was a great disappointment. I had been expecting it to be lush and tropical, as I remembered the North Queensland coast. I was so surprised by the dry streets and stark mangrove shores.

During our second year in Pine Creek, we had a minister who came down the track once a month. So everyone went to church, whether you really wanted to or not. I had never been before, so it was an interesting new experience for me.

Before I knew what was happening, I found myself teaching Sunday school. I don't know how, it wasn't easy. I learned the Catechism, the Lord's Prayer, and the words and tunes to four hymns — 'Onward Christian Soldiers', 'Abide With Me', 'There's A Home For Little Children', and 'Loving Shepherd Of My Sheep' — and I haven't improved on that since. It was all very serious. The girls were very well-behaved, while the boys sat up in the back seats of our little Church of England, and pretended to sing in Chinese. Naturally we ignored them.

Few of the Pine Creek children went on to secondary school — it was just out of the question. The exceptions were those whose parents could afford to send them to a boarding school in South Australia or

Queensland. The Stevens boys went to Charters Towers in Queensland. They would go to Darwin by train, then on to Townsville by boat, and from there catch a bus to Charters Towers. Their holidays with us came only once a year — at Christmas time. As they stepped from the train in Pine Creek, they became fair game for the local lads who wanted to play a sort of 1930s frisbee contest with their straw boater hats. Of course, both George and Fred Stevens knew the game and were able to handle the situation. It was nice to be home among friends!

Christmas and New Year was of course a time to plan for and look forward to. In the outback, where we had few holidays and special social events, it was especially exciting and we prepared for months ahead. We girls worked on doileys, tablecloths, hankies and other pretty things as gifts to put on the tree. Puddings were boiled in the copper and hung in the cool safe in their calico cloths. Cakes were made and set aside to mature — the smell of the fruit and rum seemed to fill the air in every corner of the hotel. We made sweets and biscuits until all the biscuit jars were full.

The hotel bar was closed on Christmas Day, but Mum always invited anyone around the town who had no family to come down for a meal. Later in the day friends would call in and we would exchange our little hand-made gifts. In the evening we gathered out the front with the gramophone.

New Year's Day was the time the young people would go to visit friends. A family who lived on a station outside town, asked us out there for a party. The first time my brother Ted and I went, they gave us a great day in the spirit of real bush hospitality.

The following year, we were seeing in 1931 and everyone was enjoying the party. Then someone said 'It's like last year, there are thirteen at the party — an unlucky number.' Everyone paused for a moment and shuddered, as we remembered that one of the previous

No Place for a Woman   70

year's guests, Artie Cox, had died of an illness during the year. 'Who will it be this year?' someone asked, under their breath.

Our hostess, Mrs Hardy, had sent away to a mail-order firm for a special cup and saucer, which had instructions in the art of telling fortunes by reading tea leaves left in the cup, a party game. She brought it out, thinking it would lighten up the mood and be a bit of fun. Everyone laughingly wanted their fortunes told.

When she came to my brother Ted's turn, she said, 'I'm sorry, I just can't read anything in this one,' and handed him back his cup. She told the others after we had left that it had frightened her because she clearly saw the symbol of death.

●

EARLY IN 1931, Pine Creek felt much of the excitement generated by the great England to Australia air race. Although not in Darwin to see the famous pilots and their planes land for refuelling, we watched them fly over and counted each one as they headed south. I still have autographs of Amy Johnson and of Jim Mollison, who later became her husband. Amy's came through a friend in Darwin; Jim Mollison actually visited Pine Creek and asked me to the local dance — before he married Amy of course!

The most exciting event for us was when Lieutenant Cedric Hill had a forced landing on our little strip behind the police station. Unfortunately it wasn't long enough, or he misjudged the distance. A tree stump caught on one wing, and pulled him up with a jerk. He stayed with us at the hotel, until replacement parts could be flown in for him. And Colin Cox helped Hill patch the damaged wing with parts from Anderson and Hitchcock's plane, which had crashed in 1928 at Levin Springs, seventeen miles south of Pine Creek. Keith Anderson and Bob Hitchcock had had a long association with Charles Kingsford Smith and Charles Ulm.

Anderson and Hitchcock co-piloted their small plane, the *Kookaburra*, and joined the search for their friends Kingsford Smith and Ulm when they disappeared in the West Australian desert, some years later. Sadly Anderson and Hitchcock had to make a forced landing in the desert and both perished.

My brother Ted felt very important indeed to be able to help Colin Cox and Lieutenant Hill and the hotel was a buzz of excitement. It was an event much talked about by everyone in Pine Creek for months afterwards.

Ted and I were still very close. We were alike in our looks, and had often been mistaken for twins. We had both suffered frequent bouts of malaria since coming to Pine Creek. The resident doctor from Katherine, on one of his visits to outlying settlements, called into Pine Creek, and prescribed quinine tablets — so many each day, tapering off until the course was completed. All we ever seemed to get from this was black teeth and a loud ringing in our ears.

When we had malaria, although we ran raging fevers, we also shook uncontrollably and no amount of blankets seemed to help. Mum piled them on to no avail. When the shivering stopped the sweating started, until the temperature fell. God knows how many gallons of sweat we lost. It left us totally exhausted.

Later in 1931, during one of these bouts, Ted became very ill. One night my younger brother, Jim, who was sharing a room with him, raced over to tell us that Ted was having convulsions. He seemed to be lapsing into a coma. I kept telling him that he would get better and all he could say was 'I'm all right, look after Mum, look after Mum', over and over.

Our neighbour, Mrs Jack Jones, was an Inland Mission nursing sister. She came over and said that we must get him to Darwin Hospital as soon as possible. Luckily, the train had stopped overnight in Pine Creek. In the middle of the night the crew flew into action and stoked the engine up until the boilers made enough steam. Everyone worked hard trying desperately to help. The Darwin Hospital advised they would meet the train half-way at Adelaide River with the road ambulance. Mum went with him, and we stayed behind, waiting.

Ted never came out of the coma. After two days in Darwin Hospital, he died. He was sixteen years old.

I remember every detail of the quiet Sunday when Constable Tom Turner walked into the church where I was teaching Sunday School. As soon as I looked up at him, I knew that my brother was dead. I put my book down, walked out past him, and without a word, went home. Our parents brought Ted home to bury him in our little Pine Creek cemetery. I was grief stricken. Constable Turner thought it might help me come to accept Ted's death if I was able to see his body. He was about to open the coffin so that I might see him for the last time, when someone stopped him with: 'My God, man, don't you know what you are doing? In this climate? Let her remember him in happier times.'

It was like a terrible blow to realise I would never see Ted again. It left a physical feeling of hurt where the sobs were trying to come out, and took a long time to fade away. To accept Ted's death was all the more difficult as I had managed to fight off the same illness which took his life.

· VI ·

1931–1933: LIFE GOES ON AT PINE CREEK

I LEARNT THEN the truth in the saying 'Life goes on'. I could see that our parents needed me: not just to help with all the daily work which Ted had been doing, but they were suffering terribly over the loss of their son. They grieved long and deeply. No one ever really loses this pain, but time gives you the strength to hide it from the world, and it becomes a heavy private ache that is always in your heart. We would all have moments when we were going about our daily tasks when we would be reminded unexpectedly of Ted, and tears would fill our eyes.

But we all tried hard to make the atmosphere of the hotel a happy one, despite our personal tragedy and as a way of continuing the improvements we had already started and also to keep ourselves busy, we planned and built new facilities both at the hotel and in our community.

One of the best things we did was build a tennis court. It was a great novelty in Pine Creek and was enjoyed regularly by young and old. A couple of golf holes were put down on the clear stretch of ground behind the police station (this was later used as a landing strip by Clyde Fenton, our flying doctor). Unfortunately, although we all tried, few of us made golfers but it gave us a lot of laughs. These occasions usually wound up with an evening on the grass at the hotel.

The locals still played cricket. The girls never took an active part in those days. We just sat and applauded. Looking back, I feel the game could have been upgraded with a little help from some of us young ladies — we were strong and fleet of foot.

Mum, who had always been the backbone of the hotel — ordering the stock and food, handling the wages and accounts — pushed herself through this sad time. She kept the routine going and us on our toes. Jim took over most of the jobs that Ted had done; Ethel was still at school and, like most kids her age, did as little as possible; and I tried to do as many extra tasks as I could. Having a constant working schedule in front of us each day, and knowing that we were providing a service to people, kept us all going through the first difficult months after Ted's death.

Mum worked herself so hard she must have often felt exhausted, but she never took it out on anyone by being bad-tempered or moody. She tried her best to be cheerful and loving to us — and this really helped. I would walk in and see Mum working flat-out in the kitchen, as well as managing all the other things, and I understood how hard it was for her to keep going — because grief seems to sap the usual reserves of energy. Sometimes her even temper amazed me. If the lads pinched all the cold meat which she'd made for the next day out of the cooler, she might mumble a few words, but that was it. She just set about cooking another batch. She made a habit of lying down for about twenty minutes after lunch in the quiet part of the afternoon. 'Wake me,' she would say, 'I only need these few minutes rest.'

Our menu was the same each day — steak and eggs, sausages and eggs, or bacon and eggs for breakfast; cold meats and salads for lunch; and a special dish, or roast or corned beef for dinner at night. There was always home-made soup and sweets as well. Mum never had a recipe book, but she was a good cook.

•

No Place for a Woman   76

DURING THE DRY SEASON of 1933, my brother
Jim and I, together with a girlfriend, Daphne All-
wright, drove from Pine Creek to Mt Isa. Jim was then
fifteen and Daphne and I were twenty. I think Mum
and Dad thought the trip would do us a lot of good and
help us to put the sadness of Ted's death behind us, so
they encouraged us to go.

We were travelling with Don Harkness, a Sydney engineer, who had urgent business to return to in
Sydney. He was very interested in a mining venture
in Pine Creek. Don had designed the engine of his car,
a big heavy machine that ran beautifully. He had
arranged to catch the plane at Mt Isa to travel back to
Sydney. At this time passenger aircraft only flew as
far as Mt Isa. We would drive the car back to Pine
Creek for him.

It was an adventure for us and we felt very
independent and grown-up. Daphne had never seen
sheep before as the speargrass of the Territory made
it impossible to run sheep. She kept saying: 'Look at all
that hair on those goats!' much to our amusement. At
Mt Isa Daphne and I had both had our first permanent
waves at the hairdresser and finished up looking a bit
like woolly goats ourselves!

There was a rat plague at Rankin River, on the
Barkly Tableland when we passed through. We
squashed what seemed to be thousands of them
under the tyres of the car as we drove along. At the
Rankin River Hotel, horror stories of rats' activities
didn't help us relax: they had eaten the brim off a
ringer's hat which had fallen to the floor for a minute;
and made off with a bloke's false teeth when he left
them in a glass of water overnight. We didn't hang
around.

On our way back, we retraced the route our
parents had taken when they had first come to the
Territory in 1927, six and a half years earlier. We
passed few other travellers, but felt quite safe in
Don's marvellous strong car. The dirt road was in

much better condition too, because the road workers had just been along it. It was still long and lonely but since Dad wasn't behind the wheel this time, we travelled faster!

It was fun for Daphne and I to see the reactions of everyone in Pine Creek to our new city hairdos, and we felt really refreshed by the change the opportunity for a little travel had given us.

•

I HAD COME to understand that isolation in the outback for adults meant lack of communication with the outside world. The yearning for reading material, no matter in what form, was a common one. News of any sort was read and reread: the *North Queensland Register*, the *Woman's Budget*, the Bible, the *Watch Tower*, the jam-tin label.

I started to collect reading matter and send it on to anyone who asked. Outback people told me they would read material from front to back, then back to front then check it for printer's errors for amusement, then pass it on. It was probably in circulation until it literally fell apart.

One day, Constable Tom Turner took a photograph of me and sent it with an article he wrote to a newspaper down south. He called me 'The Little Bush Maiden', and told the story of my keeping and sending reading material to outback people. We certainly didn't expect the response that we got to the article: books and papers came from all over Australia. There was not enough postage on some — which had to be taxed — and my mother must have been pretty fed up with me and my hobby, as she had to pay the tax. One batch gave our postmaster the inspiration to go artistic and he printed my name with tax stamps on a yard or so of brown paper. For me, however, it was terribly exciting and I looked forward to each mail day!

The packhorse mailman, carrying the mail between Alice Springs and Birdum during the wet season, carried on and said rude words about me when he had to put an extra horse in his team just to carry the answers to all the requests. This became a lasting joke in Pine Creek, and all along his mail route.

Mother gave me a spare room where I could put all my books and papers so I had the first free library in the north. You could browse, you could read, you could take and you could swap — just so long as you took good care of the treasure trove. I know that reading brought a great deal of pleasure to a lot of lonely people who passed through, as well as to the locals who used it regularly. Everybody talked about it and I heard myself referred to as the darling of the outback folk. Many people who came to the hotel had already heard about me, and asked to meet me. This enjoyable pursuit of mine had, to my surprise, made me known all over the outback.

•

BEFORE THE RAILWAY came to Pine Creek, mail went to and from Darwin by pony express. We read and heard wonderful tales of exciting and dangerous runs. Some of the stories about those long, lonely rides came from one of our yard men, called Jackson — a very colourful figure himself. A small and wiry Aborigine, he was a very skilled horseman and had a great sense of humour. He talked so fast in pidgin English it was hard to follow him and every second word of his vocabulary had four letters. He was very proud of the fact that he had been a pony express mailman. According to him, he rode like the wind and always delivered the mail on time, come what may — hell or high water. He rode with a rifle and had at times protected himself 'by killing a few of those Myall b . . . . . s [the wild blacks] who crossed his path' or so he said.

John Lewis was another legendary figure of earlier days in Pine Creek. He had founded the Eleanor Mine. He worked six horse-teams on the Pine Creek road, and carried machinery for the rock-crushing battery — the first in the Territory overland from Darwin. As there was no jetty at Southport, the early port for Darwin, he built one, cutting and hauling timber so that machinery could be landed from the ships.

Lewis was an experienced Pony Express rider and covered the 156 miles in a day and a night, nonstop, with a change of horses. These were frontier days, and bushrangers terrorised the Pine Creek track, so he always rode heavily armed for he frequently carried thousands of ounces of gold from the mines in his saddlebags . . .

•

I WAS A BIT OF A DREAMER and, ever since keeping my diary during our long trip in 1929, I wanted to write. I had sent some of my diary extracts off to the *Queensland Register* in Brisbane and, to my surprise, they were published. So after we went to Pine Creek, I continued to write a kind of local correspondent's report of our news for the *Register*. The outback people were always quite thrilled to see this in print when copies finally came our way.

I found that my correspondence with the *Queensland Register* was a great opportunity to gain Mother's permission to get to social events from which I might otherwise have been kept away!

One such occasion was a wedding on a small property outside town. The bride-to-be was a beautiful part-Aboriginal girl; the groom a white stockman. Of course, I was not allowed to go unchaperoned, and as no one suitable could be found, I had to stay at home. My mother knew too well what a celebration like this would be like, with all the young stockmen and their mates. So I had to resort to asking one of the station lads to make a few notes for my report.

He wrote:

The bride looked very lovely dressed in a pale pink frock and

*wearing white stockings. She carried a bunch of billy-goat
stinkers. After the wedding ceremony, the couple's four year-
old son was christened. After that we all got stuck into the
plonk and metho. It was a great party.*

I thought the 'bunch of billy-goat stinkers' a bit much,
but these little pink and white flowers (also called
'wet-the-beds') of English origin were the only flower
brave enough to bloom then, so what else could she
carry?

I believe a few of the men ended up taking pot-
shots at each other with rifles, using antbeds for
cover. Later, the groom came into town lamenting
that his bride had kicked him out of bed because he
was wearing his spurs. Also, he was uncertain about
wedding-night etiquette. Who should sleep with the
bride — the groom or the best man?

An article (not mine), printed in one Queensland
newspaper described another outback wedding, in the
course of which the bride and bridegroom had their
wedding breakfast in the hotel dining room, while the
bride's mother enjoyed hers outside on the wood-
heap. It was against the law then for an Aboriginal to
be on licensed premises.

There weren't many white women in the Territory in those days. A few lived on the cattle stations
with their husbands and families, others on the mines
or in the town; but there was a marked shortage of
single girls. For the lucky man who had a family,
outback life was great. For the lonely ones, away from
home, it must have been unbearable at times. Unless
they were very tough, most of them took up with
Aboriginal girls. The fathers and husbands of these
women would trade them for tobacco or grog. I think
some of the girls enjoyed the protection of a white
man. Many of the white men who formed these
relationships stayed with the girls and lived very full
and happy lives.

In earlier days, the children of these unions grew
up in the bush with their mothers and their families.

By the 1930s, however, the Aboriginal Protection Board had the mounted police collect them. The children with white fathers were taken from their mother, by law, when they were three or four years old, and sent to Bagot Compound or Crocker Island or Groote Eylandt missions, to be brought up as orphans. If the father of the these children recognised them, and married their Aboriginal mother (as sometimes happened), the children were not taken away. I knew some of these children who later went to boarding school in Darwin and were well educated.

●

We had a party telephone in Pine Creek, on the Darwin line. I can't remember ever 'earwigging' on Police calls, but Fanny Hayes, at Brooks Creek Railway Station often cut in on our conversations — I think she forgot at times that she should be only listening and would burst in with her threepence-worth. We would just say, 'Hey, get off the line will you!'

As a girl, I met many wonderful older women who had come to live in this hot and isolated part of Australia, to work alongside their men. They seemed to me to be a happy lot, who enjoyed their lifestyle and certainly didn't express any 'sick of their lot' stories. They worked on the stations, helping in all sorts of ways, some of them better in the saddle than any man; or at the mines, where they learned to wind a windlass, or to fell a tree and adze it for the timbering of the shafts. If you called in, the billy always seemed to be boiling for a cuppa and they always seemed to be able to produce scones, fresh bread, Johnnie cakes, or brownie from a camp oven. There was always a feed, and no traveller ever left without a freshly-stocked tucker bag.

Aunty Jess Chardon will always remain fresh in my memory. She came from Florina Station, sixty miles out of Pine Creek and wherever she went she

1918. My mother, Evelyn Pope, with her father, 'Bronco' Pope, horse-breaker.

1926. Our camp between Duchess and Mt Isa: kerosene tins and bags for the walls, dirt floor. Myself, Ted, Dad, Ethel, Jim and our beloved Rover.

1927. Crossing the Barkly. Dad checks the truck at a bore. All our belongings are on the back.

1928. Dad's gang at work on the
Katherine–Birdum railway line.

The gangers —
all hard workers.

1929. Our great trek — a stop near one
of the giant baobabs in the Kimberleys.

1929. We stop at Newcastle Waters, on our way to Alice Springs. I'm in the middle.

1929. My little sister Ethel, with Maud the doll. Home was a camp beside the road.

Alice Springs in **1929**.

Crossing the Depot sandhills, south of
Alice Springs. At times we lost sight of
the track altogether.

1929. Mrs Schunke's store at Pine
Creek — in effect the town's shopping
centre.

The Katherine baker — his name was
Crook!

1930. My mother and 'Auntie' Jess
Chardon outside the Pine Creek Hotel.

Cars in front of the Pine Creek Hotel
during the outback car rally of 1930.

Outside the Pine Creek Hotel in 1930
— you can see the accommodation block
at left. Mum, Jim, Reg Ansett, myself,
Ethel and Jack Rooney — Dad in front.

Ted and I in **1931.** The last photo of
Ted before he died.

1932. Out riding at the Copperfields.
I'm on the right.

A Pine Creek cricket match in **1932.** I'm
in the back row, left of centre, with the
upturned hat brim.

1933. Daphne and I at the Katherine
River crossing, returning from Mt Isa
— with our new perms.

A typical bushman's home. One of the
miners at the Mt Todd camp in **1933**.

My brother, Jim, in **1934.**

1935. Marlene on the old tin lizzie, on the way back to the mining camp.

Myself, with Marlene and Russell at Pine Creek in 1938.

Dad with Russell, near the old Pine
Creek Hotel in **1938.**

Joe, Marlene, myself and Warren in
Adelaide during the war.

Myself, at a picnic to Port Broughton.
We often went there on days off from
the Crystal Brook Hotel.

Beatrice in **1944**. I do not know what I would have done without her.

1945. I show Glenn how it's done, on a picnic at Port Broughton.

Everyone aboard our amphibious duck for a great day's fishing. Darwin, **1949**.

1953. The Katherine Picture Show and the Commercial Hotel in the main street of Katherine the year after I took over the hotel

In Katherine, drinkers perched like chooks on their bar stools in the hotel during the great flood of **1956.** They reckoned it was as good a place as any to sit it out.

Katherine, **1958.** I looked a lot better before the ladies race at the picnic meeting than after winning it.

Marlene, myself and Hi, Ho! Jack Davey outside the Commercial Hotel during the Redex trials.

1958. A garden party at the big white house in Katherine, to celebrate the opening of the Old Timers' Hostel.

A family group in the beer garden of the Commercial Hotel in Katherine. From left to right, my grand-daughter Yolanda, Marlene, Susanne, myself, Sandra and our friend Freddie Woods.

Myself in **1962.**

1965. Not just a good publican, a good provider as well. Barramundi and bush turkey.

Myself, posing at the entrance to the
new Pine Creek Hotel in **1968.**

1969. I often thought this was no place
for a woman either! In the kitchen at
the Pine Creek Hotel.

The Seabreeze Hotel, Darwin, 1973.
Destroyed by Cyclone Tracy in **1974.**

The old Pine Creek Hotel in **1985,** now
being restored by my daughter, Leonie.

seemed to radiate laughter and gaiety. Everyone called her aunty. She was a soft, plump lady, always beautifully dressed when she came to town, and wearing on these occasions a perfume called Black Poppy. It was so potent you could track her movements for days after her departure.

Aunty Jess often told the story of going to Florina for the first time, as a bride. The going was so rough over one of the creeks, she was bumped off the buggy and left sitting in the middle of the creek. She admitted to being 'two axe-handles across the backside', and boasted that it took two flour bags to make herself a pair of bloomers, when it only took one to make a pair for one of the black girls. Out on the isolated stations, calico flour bags were never wasted. They were washed and softened, and then sewn up into bloomers, aprons, and decorated with coloured cloth edging for house dresses. We would giggle, visualising Aunty Jess waddling around in a big pair of bloomers with 'Joe Blow's Flour' printed not only across the back but the front as well! In those days the bloomers probably wore out before the print did.

The girls on the station loved her — whenever she made the soap for the station Aunty always added sweet-smelling perfume into the mixture for them. Mind you, she had her own oil of roses for herself. It wouldn't have done to have the girls smelling the same as the missus.

Mrs Schunke lived next door to the hotel. She ran the little grocery store in the town. Her husband had owned the hotel from 1884 to 1897, so she had been in the town well over fifty years. She was already a widow when we arrived in Pine Creek, and was a lovely lavender-and-lace lady. She always had 'white help' in her beautifully-kept little house; the linen was always starched and the table set with the best silver.

My favourite was Mrs Willis. She lived near the railway line, with her husband, Ted, who worked on the railways. Mrs Willis had a crippled hand, said to have been caused by a sinew being accidentally cut when she had had an operation on it years earlier. They lived a very quiet life. Once a week I would call on her, just to say hello. She would put a white lace cloth on the table and bring out her best cups and saucers, and we would have afternoon tea. She called me Mayse mine, and I still treasure a little verse she wrote in my autograph book which reads:

I would write my name Mayse Mine,
In thy book so fine.
And when coming years bring
Changing scenes and towns
These pages scan, remember, dear,
one thou oft cheered,
with flowers and friendly chatter.
    3 December 1929

A number of our outback policemen and stockmen married Australian Inland Mission nursing sisters, or bush nurses, as they were known. So, some outback towns were blessed with a trained sister to turn to in trouble. We had Mrs Jones, a plump, jolly lady and a wonderful, capable nurse in whom we all had complete confidence.

•

THE GREAT DEPRESSION never quite hit us; or not at least to the extent it did the people down south. We did have a number of unemployed in Pine Creek, who had set up home in the railway workshop. This was a miserable place, but large and cool enough, and with plenty of water. These men received government assistance. For the sum of fifteen shillings a week, they were obliged to carry out two days' work around the town — clearing up roads and around the railway line and public buildings.

    The hotel rule was that whatever you booked up one week had to be paid before any more credit would be given. At the end of one week some of the men couldn't pay up, and Dad refused to extend their credit. This of course upset the offenders, who promptly showed their dissatisfaction by deciding to 'blacken the hotel'. (The other men, who had no problem in adhering to the rule because they still had some cash left, refused, and continued to visit the hotel.)

As for the broke ones, it was natural that they couldn't last too long without their hides beginning to crack. Our only opposition was one enterprising blackfellow, who set himself up with a box for a bar, one glass and a bottle of methylated spirits, which he sold by the nip! The next hotel was fifty miles away.

A few nights after the men had decided to blacken the hotel, the safe at the railway station was blown open, and money stolen. Then the word went out that the pub was next on the list. We waited. At night time we had to take it in turn to patrol the hotel with the shotgun. Mum and I shared one shift with Arthur Macredies, the cook at the time. We were all scared. With every noise, we asked in hoarse whispers, 'Who's there? Who's there?' If a strange voice had answered 'Me!', we would have died of fright! As it was, all our tormentors would do was lie in the ditch on the other side of the road and fire rifle shots over the top of the roof.

By the next payday the 'drought' got too much, so they called a truce, came over and paid Dad, and declared the pub open. It wasn't long, however, with the aid of a bit of Dutch courage gained over the bar, before things came to a head. The group who had blacklisted the hotel felt that the others had been traitors (and had a good time into the bargain), and should be taught a lesson.

The fight started in the billiards room. The room was unlined and when the punches flew, heads hit square-cut timber studs, and the blood flowed. The stools and billiards cues were broken and all hell broke loose. As the walls finished about three feet from the ceiling, it gave Jim, Ethel and I a good vantage point. We climbed the wall from the other side, and hung over the top of the partition, looking down at the scene below. Among the general shouts and noise, we heard someone yell, 'Get down from there, you bloody kids, before you get hurt!' But we felt safe enough, and besides, wild horses would not have dragged us away. Mum and Dad were in the bar protecting the liquor, and just had to let the brawl run its course.

Some of the men who were mere onlookers would grab a leg of a fallen hero, drag him out onto the back veranda, and hose him down with water. The drains around the hotel ran red with blood, and our bush nurse was called in to attend to the wounded.

Next day, some were limping, or on crutches, others had arms in slings, and many wore bandages on the head. It was a very sorry sight indeed. Then, as if to stir up more strife, the men decided to shift camp. They chose the local hall, a substantial old building which had once been the hospital, as their new residence. As the building had been condemned, the local constable was instructed to give them their marching orders. As he came through the gate to do his duty, he was greeted by shotgun blasts to his right and left and was told to clear off in no uncertain terms. He didn't have to be told twice. When he reported the situation to his superiors in Darwin, they told him to sit tight and wait for reinforcements.

Nine extra policemen were sent post haste from Darwin by a railway quad car. Meanwhile, back at the old hall, hurricane lamps had been hung from fence posts, and a shotgun patrol of inmates marched up and down the fence.

The policeman left them to it, and, with his wife, retired for the night. Not for long, however. We were sitting in the office at the hotel, when the dynamite went off. One end of the police station — the courthouse end — was blown sky high. Fortunately,

Constable Turner and his wife were sleeping at the other end of the building. The couple were blown out of their bed, and Mrs Turner received a nasty gash over the eye, but they were otherwise unharmed.

The constable rang the hotel for help. The regular train was on an overnight stay on its way back to Darwin, and on it were two other police constables, Jack Mahony and Bill Abbott, who were staying at the hotel. With a group of other locals, they crept around the back of the town and brought the Turners back to the hotel to safety.

After the police reinforcements arrived, the troublemakers were rounded up and things settled back to normal again.

•

WHEN THE ENTERPRISE mine reopened in the early 1930s, a couple of hundred miners moved into town. We didn't have any serious trouble with these men. They worked hard and played hard, but it was clean fun, although my mother really didn't approve. She would wake in the morning and find that her prized pot plants had been hauled up onto the roof. Or perhaps her sheets were torn and dirty after being used as capes when the lads rode pushbikes up and down the street, playing chariot races, matadors, or ghosts on the run.

There were a few near disasters when there was a misfiring at the mine. This happened when a stick of dynamite went off prematurely or, after the main blast had gone off, in a delayed explosion. I have seen men who have had clothes and boots blown off in a blast caused by one of those mishaps. The local sister had to spend quite a lot of time trying to extract small pellets of gravel out of luckless patients. One of these patients was a young fellow from Queensland, called Joe Young, and he wore little pellets of gravel under the skin on his back for the rest of his life after such an accident.

A real tragedy occurred when a young miner was shot in the stomach by a father who claimed that the boy had raped his daughter. No one ever knew if it was true or not. It was said that on his death bed, the miner denied it, so it could have been a mutual affair. The father ended up getting a life sentence for murder.

The young man was buried in the cemetery. To die here in Pine Creek was sometimes a subdued affair. If you were a pensioner, alone, without family, you could be wrapped in your blanket and laid to rest, our policeman reading a few words of respect from his Bible. The police trackers would fill in the grave and, in most cases, the name was recorded in the government *Gazette* and the police *Journal*, then forgotten.

The police station held a few coffins in readiness, but as deaths were few and far between, these were often used to hold the chook and horse feed under the police station. There were long coffins and short coffins and, if you were unlucky enough to be tall and to need one when only a short job was available, then a small operation had to be done to your legs. To handle this, the 'surgeon', who was the local policeman, first spent a couple of hours in Dowling's bar. This helped anaesthetise him. A bit gruesome, perhaps, but it was a duty expected of the police in those days.

I must add, that if peace and quiet was what was wanted, you would find it there in the Pine Creek cemetery. The only noise to break the silence would be the chatter of the birds, mostly parrots, and the Happy Family, or Apostle birds, who do make a din, or the thud of hooves from stray cattle, horses, or buffalo.

•

ALTHOUGH YOU CAN NEVER really get over the loss of a child, time had healed our parents a little, and I could see that they had begun to accept Ted's death.

Mum's good humour had returned and once again she managed to add a little fun to her chores. The gramophone played overtime. One of her favourite tunes was the old 'Black and White Rag'. If she was mopping the floor she would dance and skip around with the mop as her partner, humming along with the bright catchy tune.

We made our own fun, as all small places do. We held dances in the local hall, and these were special occasions we young ones looked forward to. There was a piano, but if no player was available, there was always the Dowling gramophone. We also had a bass made from a tea chest with strings tied to a broom handle, and a stick with beer-bottle tops tacked over it. Among the local equipment we could draw on was a scrubbing board, a jew's harp, accordion, banjo, mandolin, ukulele, violin, and mouth organ, and, of course, singers — it's surprising what talent could be found in the sparsely populated outback.

I loved to dress up, and took great interest in designing myself new outfits and hairstyles for these occasions. Our friend Mrs Finness was a good dressmaker, and I would order fabrics from down south, and then draw the designs for her to make up for me.

We would arrange special occasions, such as fancy dress. On other nights you might be asked to wear something representing the title of a song. Prizes were given, which would be some nice little home-made gift; the booby prize could be a box of wrapping paper tied up with ribbon containing a clothes peg or a roll of toilet paper or bunch of billy-goat stinkers.

I remember one night when all the ladies had to put one shoe in a bag. It was a sort of lucky dip — or unlucky dip. The fellow had to find the pair to the shoe he had drawn out and dance with its owner. My mother was left with one shoe on and no partner. We later found her other shoe behind the piano. Just as well she was a good sport!

At the hotel, we had reason to show off when we acquired the first ice-making plant in Pine Creek. It was a thing of wonder for us all, but the ice didn't come out in nice square blocks. The contraption consisted of a long length of pipe with a large ball on each end. The ball at one end was held over a flame until it was red-hot, and then it was plunged into cold water. This caused a chemical reaction, by some miracle which we didn't quite understand, to freeze up the other ball, covering it with frost before our eyes. This icy ball was fitted into a cold box, and we had our beer cooler.

A few years later, some con-man talked Mum into setting up a lot of car batteries, which were supposed to run a small refrigerated cool room to do the same job on a bigger scale. Either the workings were too complicated for our simple minds, or the salesman recognised a couple of 'live ones' when he saw them. Anyway, he made good use of his luck, and the fact that he'd be long gone by the time we'd figured out that the system didn't work!

· VII ·

1933–1942: BACK TO CAMP FIRE
COOKING

A S I G R E W U P, my life still centred at the
hotel, where people were always socialising, so
although I was working I met everyone who came to
town. I mixed easily, and lots of group activities were
arranged for the young people — picnics, tennis,
dances (at which my mother always chaperoned me).
A lot of the boys paid me attention, but I never really
fell in love with any of them. All of us who had grown
up together in Pine Creek were like brothers and
sisters, and it needed an outsider to attract our
romantic attention.

My mother never really discussed love or marriage with me. I don't think any of the mothers
thought to discuss these things with their girls in
those days. They grew up in the Victorian era, and
were never told anything themselves. Naturally they
did not know how to talk these things over with their
own daughters. My girlfriends and I didn't discuss it
much either. We all just expected that one day we
would fall in love with a Prince Charming, and marry.
We never questioned what our life would be like after
marriage.

In 1932, Joe Young came to the Pine Creek area
looking for work in the mines. He had driven over
from Queensland with a couple of mates, and the
three of them frequented the hotel. They all paid me
attention, and although the other two asked me out, it

was Joe's quiet, understated attention that won me over. He was six feet tall, dark and handsome, and always a gentleman — although very shy — which all the women found charming. We became friends, and it stayed that way for a long time, until I realised our friendship had become a courtship.

When it came to courting in Pine Creek, there wasn't much opportunity for romance in the glamorous sense. There were the occasional dances and picnics, but the regular social activity in the evenings was to sit around the gramophone at the hotel. In those days everyone accepted that young people conducted their courtship in the company of their friends and often under the watchful eyes of their parents, too.

Joe was rather persuasive, bringing me in bush orchids or bunches of wild flowers; I was always touched by this and by his diffidence when he presented them to me. When in 1933 he asked me to marry him, I accepted.

Joe seemed like a very dependable man to me. He was very strong and a tireless worker, and he had a good sense of humour. He was what people call a man's man. Although he had a quiet manner with women, he would come out of himself in the company of his mates, and be outgoing and quite boisterous at times, although he only drank light shandies and never smoked. He was a great practical joker, and created an uproar in the bar with pranks such as unravelling the puggaree on an unsuspecting drinker's pith helmet and letting the rim down around his neck.

Although they never said it, Mum and Dad were a little disappointed that I was marrying a miner. They knew it was a hard life, and I think they had hoped I might meet someone who could have promised a more secure financial future. Mum's parents probably thought the same thing when she married Dad, a railway worker.

As a young woman I had dreamed about getting married and making a life of my own. As the day approached, however, my excitement was mixed with a strange feeling of anxiety. It was sad to realise that I might not have my mother there when I needed her in future. She was my best friend. And the prospect of moving out to live at the remote Spring Hill Mine, where Joe worked, away from the stimulating life of the hotel and my family and friends, was a little daunting. I knew that there were no other women at the mine, but I wanted to be with Joe, and in becoming his wife, I accepted that from now on I would have to be prepared to live wherever he could find work.

In those mid-Depression years, few people had big weddings, and as none of Joe's people could come, we decided to make ours a simple occasion. It was a morning wedding in the little Pine Creek Church. I wore an ankle-length cream cotton and lace dress with a small hat, and carried a bouquet of frangipani. Joe wore his best white duck suit which was still high fashion for men. Our guests were my family and a few close friends. We walked back to the hotel for the wedding breakfast, which my mother and Mrs McNiece had prepared. Although the miners in Pine Creek came to accept the locals as their family, I felt Joe was a little saddened that none of his people, especially his mother, could be there. He had written to tell her about me, and sent a photo, but it was not until years later that we actually met.

His father had been killed at Gallipoli when Joe was nine years old, and as he was the oldest in his family, he had gone out to work at a very young age as a billy boy for a road gang in the Adelaide Hills. All his single life, and for a long time after we were married, he always sent home money to help his mother.

When we were married, Joe had very little money and was working hard. That didn't bother me. My own parents were battlers, and I could see how they had built up a family business from nothing over the years. We were young and healthy, and we planned to build up our savings and eventually have a home of our own in Pine Creek. At twenty, I felt more than ready to be married and start a family of my own.

We couldn't afford a honeymoon, so a couple of days after the wedding we packed our things into Joe's old truck and bumped our way along the twenty miles of dirt road to the Spring Hill Mine, north of Pine Creek. When we got there, my first home greeted me: a fibro and iron hut — two rooms with a veranda along the side. It was quite an establishment by bush mining camp standards.

It was a challenge for me to make the place a little more liveable, so I set to work with gusto, easily remembering all the camping routines learned from Mother during our years of tent living. It took only a day or two to get things into shape, as we had the barest essentials for bush living. Then, time began to drag. I was the only woman living on the mine, and the sudden change from the busy comings and goings at the hotel took a bit of adjusting to. I focused my attention on observing the bush and daydreaming for hours, as I had done as a girl at Maranboy.

It wasn't very long before I started to wake up feeling decidedly sick each morning, and the smell of the corned beef cooking was often enough to make me ill. Although I didn't know all that much about pregnancy, it occurred to me that it was a possibility. When we next went back to town for supplies and I told my mother, she took me down to see Mrs Jones, the bush nurse, who confirmed I was having a baby.

I didn't return to the mines with Joe, as the wet season was closing in, and I could have been cut off in case of any emergency. I was quite relieved to remain at the hotel where I was within reach of the bush nurse, and once again able to enjoy the company of my mother and friends.

Then, my parents and Joe talked me into going south for my confinement. They thought it would be a lot safer, and Mrs McNiece said that her sister in Melbourne would be glad to have me stay with her until the baby was born. This was not unusual for Territory women in those days, especially for a first baby.

When I was about seven months pregnant, I boarded the train at Pine Creek with Joe, who came with me as far as Darwin. I waved goodbye to my parents with a sinking feeling in my heart. I had never been parted from my family before and when Joe and I said our goodbyes and I boarded the boat in Darwin, bound for Melbourne, I felt overwhelmed by loneliness. Just at the time when having a mother and friends around me could have been such a comfort and help, I was to be in a strange city with strangers caring for me.

Added to this, I was extremely seasick. When we docked at Brisbane, an old friend of the family met me with a beautiful bunch of flowers. I had not seen such exotic flowers since I was a child at Ingham School. Their perfume and beauty touched a nostalgic trigger, and I made a show of myself and sobbed and sobbed.

Mrs McNiece's sister, June, met me in Melbourne. She put her arm around me and greeted me warmly. I was so grateful to put my feet on solid ground and get over my constant sea sickness, that at first I was hardly aware of the city itself. June and her husband lived in St Kilda, and I settled in to wait the five weeks for the baby to arrive. Although everyone was very kind to me I often felt lonely, and filled in the days with making baby clothes and writing letters home.

It was the height of the Great Depression in Melbourne, and it seemed to have touched everyone. Visitors and friends to June's house spoke of having to stand in line with their ration cards for meat — which they said was often not fit for a dog and sometimes nearly rotten. But they had to take it or go without. It seemed particularly sad for me when as I said in my letters home, in the cattle country I knew we had plenty of fresh meat.

Like most 'bushies' going to a city, Melbourne held many wonders for me. We went sightseeing to the beach and on a few shopping expeditions to the city when I felt better, and I found the sophistication and bustle exciting, although a little frightening. All the window shopping must have gone to my head, because I impulsively lashed out and spent twenty-two pounds (most of my savings from my hotel days) on a bedroom suite. As we only had the bark hut at the time, it must have seemed ridiculous to Joe and Mum, who nearly had a fit at the freight bill, but it was my way of making a nest to take my baby home to.

For my confinement I went into a private hospital, and was attended by a doctor. I did not know anything much at all about what lay ahead of me. My mother had not told me anything. I found out for myself — and how! I did not have what was called a complicated labour, but towards the end, I thought I was going to die. Then, finally, it was over and they brought a blonde blue eyed baby girl for me to hold. I was so convinced that my baby was going to be dark haired like Joe that I said, 'That's not my baby!' The doctor said, 'It's got to be. This is the only baby in the hospital!'

I stayed on with June until Marlene was six weeks old and able to travel. I counted the days until I could get back home. Knowing how hard it had been for me, and how anxious I was to get back to my family, Mum and Dad paid my return airfare. I flew back north by Qantas Airways to Daly Waters. At that time Marlene was the youngest passenger they had carried to the Northern Territory and they made a great fuss of us.

On the dusty outback airstrip at Daly Waters, Joe met us and saw his daughter for the first time. I suddenly felt enormous relief to be back home again, and the tears came flooding out. We stayed that night at the Daly Waters pub and drove the 200 miles back up to Pine Creek the next day, where Marlene received a great welcome from her grandparents and family.

●

MARLENE WAS ONLY a few months old when we went to live out at the gold mine at Spring Hill again. Joe had been contracted to drive a tunnel into the side of the hill for the mines company. He worked long hours during the day and at night, because it was cooler too, darn near killing himself. Only the heat and the lack of air in the tunnel forced him to take a break.

I was still the only woman out there. We had to carry our water in buckets and cook over an open fire. It was hard work with a small baby to care for. At night candles and hurricane lamps were our only lighting, and I felt very isolated in the surrounding darkness, alone with the baby when Joe was in the tunnel. The dingoes would prowl and howl around the back door, foraging in the garbage, I wasn't really frightened, but I hated it. I would sit and hold my baby and wait for him to come home.

I was homesick and lonely for the life of the hotel and my family around me, so to keep the peace, we would go into town every couple of weeks. It was also an excuse to take a pile of washing in to do under easier conditions.

As we only had an old rattletrap Tin Lizzie, held together with odd bits and pieces, we broke down often on these trips. When this happened, we had to camp beside the road. It meant collecting all the available manure — horse, cow, buffalo — to make smoke fires to keep the mosquitoes at bay. It didn't take us long to get smart and carry swags, mosquito nets, plenty of water and a tucker box.

While I was at Spring Hill, a young mother came

out to see me. She was a friend who had hopped on the train at Pine Creek and got off at the Spring Creek siding, especially to find me. She said she felt she had no one else to turn to. She had a very tiny baby and was at her wits' end, he just cried and cried. She was breast-feeding him, but it was easy to see that there wasn't enough nourishment in her milk to satisfy him. My knowledge of babies was pretty slight too, but I did the only reasonable thing I could think of: I breast fed him myself — luckily I had plenty of milk. After a good tuck-in, he went to sleep. No doubt it was the first decent feed he'd had in some time. I kept him fed until we could get in to Pine Creek, where the 'old hands' showed the mother how to make up a bottle to help supplement her milk.

When the wet season set in in 1934, we left Spring Hill for the Mt Todd Gold Mine, south of Pine Creek, where Joe had organised another job. We went back into Pine Creek for a few days to get our gear and stores ready and packed it all into the old Ford tin Lizzie. My brother, Jim, aged eighteen, decided to come out with us to work at the mine.

The road out to Mt Todd was very difficult. We followed the old telegraph road, which was then a rough bush track. We crossed the Cullen River about fifteen miles from Pine Creek, but when we arrived at the Ferguson River, a further five miles on, we found it to be running a very strong 'banker', swirling along logs and debris, the water brown and muddy-looking.

Although there were crocodiles in the Ferguson River, we had to get across. The most important part of the truck was the carburettor, to be kept dry at all costs. It was chain-driven, one of Joe's inventions and the pride of his heart, so we took it off. We decided to rig up a windlass to a tree across the river and as Joe was the strongest swimmer, he was the one chosen to swim over with the rope. He went upstream to enter the water and swam down with the current, coming out the other side. Once there, he took the tow rope that he had tied to his waist and set up the windlass around a good sturdy tree, then, inch by inch, the truck was winched across the river.

At one point it was completely submerged in the water, and we thought we were going to lose it. Any of the gear which hadn't been tied down firmly started to leave the load: my saucepans, a tin of our precious petrol and Jim's pumpkin came out of his tucker box and floated away. You would have thought that pumpkin was made of gold, the fuss he made.

We had carried cases of clothes and a swag across the railway bridge before winching the truck over. I walked over the bridge, stepping from sleeper to sleeper carrying the baby. It was a very high bridge, and wasn't for the faint-hearted!

Once we were over the Ferguson, the engine dried off and we were ready for the road again. The old road had been bad enough but once we left it, the dirt track was even more treacherous. It was like a nightmare; we had seventeen more miles to travel and there were times when I really felt we wouldn't make it, especially when it became dark and we had only one headlight, and that not too bright. The Ferguson crossing hadn't helped the brakes — we had none.

We finally arrived. Waiting for us was a bark hut. At least it was dry. On a previous visit, Joe and some boys working for him had made it out of saplings and sheets of paperbark — this formed a roof and walls for one room, with an open veranda for living and kitchen adjoining it. The floors were packed earth, I cooked on an open fireplace outside, and our furniture was made of saplings and kerosene cases. This was my new home.

Next morning we unloaded all my boxes and dried out the wet gear under the veranda. Joe left for work and I was alone again with the baby. The hut was out of sight of the mine and I couldn't see a friendly thing, not even another tent. The strips of bark on the walls were burnt black in parts, just as though they had been peeled from the trees after a bushfire had passed through, and they presented a very dismal sight. At that moment our house presented no challenge to me. I was wet, lonely and very sorry for myself. I just sat on a kerosene case, fed the baby and had a bloody good howl.

Of course I was used to bush living, and it wasn't long before I pulled myself together and had a fire going and the billy on. I made two big mosquito nets, using double sheets for the top and green net for the drops. One I used to cover the beds, and the other was hung over the table, so we could eat in peace. We made a safe cot for the baby: one completely covered with fly wire with a lift-up top and drop sides, so that Marlene played safely and happily. When the humidity was very high and she developed prickly heat, I hung wet towels around her cot to help cool her down.

Joe later found a little wood stove for me, and this was a great help. I could make bread and cakes, and as I was the only woman living at the mine, we often had visitors in the evenings for a chat and a snack.

. The day I baked my first loaf of bread I was so proud, I ran all the way to the mine to show it off!

We would send in our order to the railway store in Darwin and our supplies came weekly by train to the Edith River siding. We collected them by truck and on packhorses. We had to cart water to the camp. Every now and then, one of the boys would come up and chop a heap of firewood for me. Other than that, I had no use for help.

We had a Coolgardie safe to help keep the food cool, but there was no way we could keep fresh meat. One of the local stations ran a beast in once a fortnight and killed it at the mine site, and then we had fresh meat for two days. The rest we salted and hung in bags in a shed covered in hessian to keep the flies off it. This salt junk, as we called it, had to be soaked overnight in water before cooking. It was good meat, and it is amazing how many dishes you can create out of a lump of corned beef — curry, stew, mince, rissoles, shepherd's pie, spaghetti, meat pie, burdekin duck — to name a few.

In our wanderings, wherever we made camp one of the first things I did was pick a bunch of wild flowers, and if we were to be there a month or so, I would dig a plot and plant my radish seeds. They germinated quickly and you could be eating them about three weeks later. I used them in salads, stews, whatever was cooking. An old timer had once said to me 'Don't bother growing flowers, Missus. If you can't eat the bloody things, don't grow them!' and I took his advice.

It didn't take long for the old bark hut to become home. The antbed floor set hard and was easy to keep clean. I had creek ferns growing in hollow logs around the veranda area. The kerosene cases turned into seats and cupboards, and covered with some bright cretonne looked very homely.

The days seemed to pass quickly in the bush. We went early to bed, as there wasn't much pleasure in reading by the light of the hurricane lamp; these seemed to draw the creepy crawlies like a magnet. In the evenings we often sat around a camp fire, which may sound silly in the tropics, but there is nothing friendlier than an open fire. It can be great company — and when you are alone just to sit and stoke the blaze and watch a billy of tea brewing on the side cheers you up. At dusk we enjoyed many good times, sitting having a 'wongie' (talk) or swimming in the river.

When I first arrived the blacks visited our camp, naked as the day they were born, except for a brief lap-lap or narga. Marlene was fascinated by the bare behinds. Bums, bums, she kept saying. In turn, they seemed to be fascinated with her blonde curly hair. I gave them damper when I had any and some of Joe's old shorts.

On weekends, we would sometimes venture further into the bush to explore. Ours was the first motor vehicle to get to the Mt Todd Falls. We had to break our own track and the going was very tough. The trees were no problem to knock down or dodge, but the boulders were more serious. Our Aboriginal guide would only go a certain distance with us because he was afraid of the rainbow snake which, he swore, lived in the waterhole under the falls.

After that we went there often for picnics, as it was such a beautiful place. We camped there one night during a bad thunderstorm. The noise seemed to echo around the ironstone cliffs, and the lightning turned the valley into continuous daylight.

Strange as it might seem, I cried the day I left the old bark hut. We had been living at Mt Todd for close on twelve months, and I had made it home. I was sad leaving my packing-case furniture and little garden.

Work had cut out at the mine, so we headed back to Pine Creek and stayed with my parents at the hotel for a while. By then I was pregnant with my second child and Marlene was nearly two. Joe got work with the overland telegraph company, and we moved up to Darwin. Jim bought himself a truck with his savings, and came up to join us, working as a carrier.

•

OUR HOUSE IN DARWIN was our first real home since we were married. It overlooked Vestey's Beach, from the top of the cliffs at Bullocky Point. It was a lovely spot. Our only neighbouring house was used to accommodate the Qantas Airways pilots during their overnight stay in Darwin. This was managed by a wonderful happy lady, Mrs Ray, fondly called Mum Ray by all those who knew her.

Mum would often go with us to the pictures on

Saturday nights. She would get herself all ready as far as her petticoat, leaving her dress to slip on at the last minute. She would wear a large apron while she got the boys — her pilots — their evening meal. One night they were late getting in to Darwin, and held her up. Joe, never known for his patience, was tooting the horn 'to liven her up'. Mum Ray raced out, hopped in the car and it wasn't until we were going into the theatre that she realised she had forgotten to put her dress on! We offered to take her back home, but she just laughed and said: 'They'll think I'm in my evening gown anyhow!' and went on in!

I ought to mention that in those days it was formal wear at the Star Theatre — long evening gowns for the ladies and white duck suits for the men. It was a glamorous affair. Upstairs was 'Whites Only', but as Mum Ray couldn't walk up the stairs because of her bad legs, she always sat downstairs and reckoned she had some good mates there anyhow.

In Darwin blacks and whites were separated both by social custom and by law. It was a gaol offence to consort with an Aboriginal after dark or to supply him or her with alcohol.

In mid-1936, Joe went into training for a big boxing match. He had a reputation as a bare-knuckle fighter — he had boxed and wrestled professionally in Queensland when he was younger and was talked into taking on the Darwin champion, Goldie Tybell. Some of Goldie's fans had thrown out the challenge. Although my mother always said that Joe would sooner have a good fight than a feed, I don't think he really wanted to fight Goldie, but his masculine pride would not let him back down. Training was solid work. He boxed, skipped and ran the length of Mindle Beach ankle-deep in water every night. I was his only coach. Very pregnant, I just sat on a rock and enjoyed the view!

I went to the fight (still very pregnant). It was quite an event and drew a big crowd — Darwin men loved a good fight. It was held in a large hall with a raised ring, ropes, a formal referee and judges, with a lot of betting going on on the sides. And knowing Joe, although he never admitted it, I'm sure he had a side bet on himself. The fight only went one round. Joe had said it would go to the second, but something upset him and he knocked Goldie cold — much to my relief and the uproar of the crowd.

I was glad when it was over. I had seen hundreds of pub brawls, but this was my first professional fight. Goldie recovered and became one of Joe's best mates — a friendship which lasted a lifetime.

Overnight, Joe — Bogger as he was known — became the hero of Darwin. In October, our son Russell arrived and even the Aboriginal girl who helped me with him when I brought him home, would sing to him a little tune that went, 'Wudgell James, Wudgell James Young, you gonna be fighter alla same your Daddy!'

Not long after this Joe decided to take a miner's job again and we moved back to Pine Creek. We built a lovely new house there, intending it to be our permanent home. But in the late 1930s work was very scarce in the Pine Creek area and we were forced back to Darwin. Moving had become a way of life for me so I just accepted it. After all, we all depended on Joe as our breadwinner and he had to go where the work was.

In 1938, at the beginning of the wet season, Tom Cole, our buffalo shooter friend, gave us his one ton-truck to use while we were in Darwin. Tom said it was better than having it jacked up and idle in the wet season. So we pulled the Pine Creek house down, planning to re-erect it on a block of land we had bought in Darwin. In the meantime, we had a shed fixed up and made liveable at the back of the block, and moved into that. I was back to living in camp-like conditions, with two small children and another on the way.

Joe put a five-hundred gallon ship's tank on the back of Tom's truck and, with a contract he had from the old Terminus Hotel, he would bail water from the Parap Dam with a bucket, and fill the hotel water tanks. He worked very hard, but it brought in good money. He was soon able to afford another tank, then a small pump. It wasn't long before he had a bigger truck and he branched out into carting sand as well. In those days, if you made yourself a road into a sandpit, it was considered yours. If you poached, as one chap did in Joe's pit, you could quite easily finish up with a fat lip, a black eye and a few stitches for good measure. The trucking business grew, and we acquired more and bigger vehicles. They carted beer to the hotels, and goods from the bond store at the wharves.

The dismantled house from Pine Creek had never been re-erected, so we had purchased another house near the Daly Street Bridge. It had a few more mod cons than the shed — the main one was running water! Seven months pregnant, I was finding pulling up the bucket from the well a bit much.

Unfortunately the people occupying the house refused to get out. An eviction order had no effect. Joe moved in too, but was ordered off. The only time he was allowed there was to collect the rent and the occupiers stayed on until they were good and ready to leave. By this time my waiting was over, the baby was due to arrive and we still had no house, so Joe rallied his mates and got the Pine Creek house up by the time I came out of hospital. It was a lovely place — up on stilts, so it was cool and comfortable; it had polished wooden floors and a nice big kitchen. I wouldn't have called the Queen my Aunty, I was so proud of it.

Our third child, Warren, was born in Darwin Hospital. The night he arrived I went to the pictures and sat next to my doctor. When he asked me how I was feeling, I said, 'Fine, I'm just filling in time, I'll be going to hospital after the show'.

We were now an established family with our

three beautiful children: Marlene with her mop of blonde curls was very pretty and gentle; Russell, also fair, was a serious, placid little boy; Warren, dark-haired, with dark brown eyes, was a merry little mischief, loved by everyone, and he ruled Beatrice, our helper, who was a Groote Eylandt girl, part-Aboriginal. I had met her when she was a nursemaid for a friend. When that family moved south, Beatrice went back to the Bagot Compound where she did washing and ironing and made children's clothes. She asked the matron, whom I knew well, if she could come to work for me.

Beatrice was a deeply religious girl, very clean and happy, and hard-working. She loved my children, and they loved her. She was part of our family for over eighteen years, and in all that time we never exchanged a cross word.

Joe had plenty of work now, and we were able to furnish our home with nice things. I even had my own car to take Marlene to and from school each day. But it was all too good to last. By 1941, Australian soldiers were visible in Darwin, and the news of the conflict in the Pacific was bringing the Second World War uncomfortably close.

●

TRUCKS AND SOLDIERS poured into Darwin. Men marched up and down the roads and around the streets. Darwin women weren't used to being whistled at by strangers — the shortage of girls in the Territory meant anything in a skirt was fair game.

There was a sense of tension, but none of us anticipated any real action on Australian soil. Then came practice air raid alerts. When the sirens screamed their warnings, it was gather your children together, grab your bags and get to the nearest shelter. We dug our slit trenches in the back yard and had a bag packed and ready on the back veranda with food, mosquito nets, water, and the essentials needed in a hurry.

As the Japanese threat grew, we were given the order to evacuate. Women and children, invalids, and the aged were moved south from Darwin in December, 1941. Most went willingly, but some refused. Boatloads of families left Darwin harbour for southern cities and safety; some were turned back after reportedly sighting Japanese submarines. Many of these boats were short on space and lifeboats. For this reason, Joe refused to let us go.

I was given twenty-four hours to pack my bags and get ready. Joe said that if anyone came back pestering us, he would throw them down the stairs by the seat of their pants. The army said if we were attacked they wouldn't be responsible for us and with that, they left us alone and I stayed on.

On 11 December, 1941, the warning sirens sounded in earnest for the first time. There was no moon, most residents had gone to bed. Air-raid wardens patrolled their beats, yelling to people to 'put out their bloody lights', smashing windows to put out lights in empty houses, giving advice on where to go and what to do in urgent voices.

Those people who were still in the streets headed for the beach and huddled there to be eaten alive by mosquitoes and sandflies. Those who were at home grabbed their blankets, pillows, mosquito nets and water, and with their families crouched in their 'funk holes', waiting for the sounds of the anti-aircraft fire which would herald the start of the raid. Huddling in a slit trench with my loved ones was as close as I would ever want to be to war. Waiting and not knowing what was to happen was terrifying.

Nearly nine hours later the all clear was sounded. The enemy had not appeared, and we later learned that it was the daylight hours which would be the most dangerous, as the carrier-borne aircraft did not take off at night. After this alarm, thousands of soldiers spent Christmas and New Year erecting barbed wire entanglements along the beaches.

Christmas 1941 came and went with no celebration, even for the children. I now realised we had to get out of Darwin, as a Japanese attack might come at any moment. The last few days were tense and frightening: listening for the sounds of the warning sirens and waiting for news of a place on an evacuation flight.

· VIII ·

1942–1945: THE WAR YEARS

ON NEW YEAR'S Eve, 1941, I was lucky enough to get a flight out of Darwin, and we arrived in Adelaide on New Year's Day, 1942. Joe and my brother Jim stayed behind to help with essential services. Joe used his earth-moving plant to build airstrips near Darwin. The children and I, with our single small suitcase of clothes, had left our lovely home with all its new furniture, and all our worldly goods — wedding presents, irreplaceable personal treasures, old and new.

When we left Darwin all we could take with us were the barest of necessities; everything else had to be left behind, and no arrangements were made to safeguard our property. Apparently it was not the business of the Commonwealth Government to protect people's belongings. Through my tears I kept trying to convince myself that we were lucky to be alive and together, and I should not be worrying about possessions.

I had identification bracelets made for each of the children to wear in case we were ever separated. Beatrice stayed with us in Adelaide. The head of the Department of Aboriginal Affairs at the time of the evacuation was also a friend, and he knew me well enough to allow me to keep her with my family knowing she would be well looked after. With the help of Joe's mother we rented a house in Adelaide. Prior to the evacuation, Mum and Dad had taken

Marlene and my younger brother, Keith, for a holiday in Sydney. When we were flown to Adelaide, they came straight over to join us. Seeing Dad again was a comfort, it was nice to have a man in the house with us, and the children were glad to be reunited.

Barely two days after I left, Darwin had a second serious alert. Six weeks later on 19 February 1942, Japanese bombers and fighters ripped Darwin apart. There was panic and terror. People fled by any means, with whatever they could gather up quickly.

Even though we had half-expected it, the first shock of the news was devastating. We were all concerned for friends and family who were still up there. Joe was working out of Darwin at the time of the raid, although I did not find that out until later. We had to wait for news over the wireless and through the papers. We finally found out through the army that both he and Jim were unhurt. During the time we were separated, Joe worked hard and played hard with his mates — drinking, gambling and playing practical jokes. He nevertheless remained very popular!

Approximately seven hundred people were killed or injured in the raid. At first the press tried to tell us that only nine people were killed, but we knew this was wrong. Almost all the vessels in the harbour — including American warships — were destroyed, and all the prominent buildings and virtually the whole central business district of the city were bombed, all in one daylight air attack.

My friend Doug Lockwood, the author, in his book *Australia's Pearl Harbor*, quoted the Japanese Commander Fuchida, who said: 'The harbour was crowded with all kinds of ships which we picked off at our leisure.'

Darwin was bombed on fifty-eight other occasions between March 1942 and 12 November 1943. Some were nuisance raids by just two or three aircraft, but many were full scale attacks by a large number of bombers. The Australian Government responded by sending men north. It was said that by 1943 our military strength between Darwin and Mataranka had risen to more than 50 000 men.

Joe wanted to join the commandos, but unfortunately a shooting accident some years earlier had severely damaged one of his arms, and he was rejected by the army. He worked with his road construction plant, assisting with the construction of the Stuart Highway, until the Government impressed his equipment, which left him no other choice but to join us in the south. It was a bitter blow to him, losing the plant which had taken him so long to build up. The Darwin Acquisition Act also took our freehold blocks of land in Darwin, which were quite extensive. We had just completed a house on one of them for my parents' retirement in Darwin. Eventually they intended to lease the Pine Creek Hotel.

•

OUR RENTED HOUSE was in the Adelaide suburb of Dulwich. However, when the owners returned from holidays they were annoyed to find we had small children. They made things a bit unpleasant for me, by calling every other day to make sure the children hadn't been riding stick horses that would leave marks on the gravel driveway!

Indoor living was difficult for us all, too. My mother-in-law insisted that the blinds be kept closed in case the sun faded the curtains and furniture. The inside of the house looked like the Black Hole of Calcutta. We had to keep the lights on to see! None of us had ever dealt with a chip heater before. The first time it burst into flames I nearly went through the roof. Ma-in-law kept saying 'Don't be silly, Mayse knows how to light a chip heater,' but Mayse had no idea. A bigger bunch of country bumpkins never hit Adelaide.

Beatrice would sit out in the back yard minding

the children, while I prepared the meals. Then I took over with the children, while she cleaned up. It was a miserable existence. Not far from us was an asylum. Whenever the sirens went off there (we never understood why), the children thought they were back in Darwin and would make a dash for the kitchen table to take cover. One bonus for living in Adelaide was the nectarine tree in the back yard. We had never tasted nectarines before, and the tree laden with beautiful fruit gave us some wonderful feasts. Also, at the shops we discovered fruits which we could never get in the tropics, and which were so cheap to buy — cherries, grapes, peaches, apricots — there were a few tummyaches in our house!

We went for rides on the trams and the children loved the novelty. Marlene and Russell were blonde like me, but Warren had taken after his dark-eyed dad and everywhere we went Warren would run to me, and then to Beatrice. You could see people wondering if he belonged to me or to her.

We went to the beautiful Botanic Gardens and the zoo, and for rides on 'Popeye', the ferry that cruised up the Torrens River. This was not just an exciting event for the children — we all enjoyed these first-time treats too.

Joe began to look into leasing a hotel as a business for the family, and we finally settled for the Railway Hotel in Crystal Brook — a town a little over one hundred miles out of Adelaide, and about thirty miles from Port Pirie.

We took it sight unseen, and were very relieved to find it was quite a big building and, importantly for the children, it had lots of space around it. Joined to the main building by a wide, covered breezeway was a four-roomed cottage. We shared this with my parents. Beatrice had her own room close by. We quickly made the place feel like home.

The liquor stock was limited by the wartime quota system. We were soon swapping and trading with the other hotels — wine for beer and that sort of thing — and managed quite well. The lemon essence, which was pure alcohol, wasn't safe from the girls in the kitchen! Mixed with lemonade, it made a potent brew. All shandies for the lady drinkers were non-alcoholic, made from Bosther Beer and lemonade to save the beer supply, but they still seemed to get the giggles.

Crystal Brook held one of the biggest livestock auctions outside Adelaide and on sale days the streets would be lined with expensive cars. I always felt that the buyers not only bought a cut lunch with them, they also turned their sixpences over a couple of times before buying a drink. We weren't destined to make our fortune in Crystal Brook.

Most of the local ladies still looked the other way when passing the hotel. One of the 'nicer' women had an afternoon tea party to introduce me to the others. It was a lovely spread, set out in one of their houses, but you could have cut the atmosphere with a knife. I felt like a strange creature on show. I am sure they thought that because I was the licensee of a hotel, I was a scarlet women. I felt like saying, 'I wouldn't mind looking at the skeletons in your cupboards, you sanctimonious bitches!'

One woman actually came to the back of the hotel and asked if I would supply her with a flagon of wine at the same price as the previous licensee, and could I have my 'boots' deliver it — after dark, of course — and leave it at her back door. And would I mind not walking her to the back gate of the hotel yard, in case someone should see me talking to her? Coming from Darwin, where I had moved with the upper crust, so to speak, it was hard to understand this kind of small town snobbery.

We lived a busy life in the hotel. Beatrice joined the local church. After she sang the first few bars of a hymn in her deep contralto voice, the congregation stopped and turned around to look at the new member and took her under their wing. When we left Crystal Brook they presented her with a lovely blue travelling case as a going-away gift.

We knew that all our friends had been evacuated from Darwin and news filtered through all the time about what was happening up north. A number of Territory people visited us at Crystal Brook. We were all sad and worried, and very anxious to be allowed to return.

One of the women who had refused to move out of Darwin with the first evacuation was dear old Aunty Jess Chardon, who'd gone there to live after leaving Florina Station. Like many other Darwinites, she looked up into the sky during the main attack, saw objects falling out of planes and thought they were propaganda leaflets. It was only when the first bombs started exploding that she reacted. She was out on her veranda having a cuppa at the time and, as she recounted it, she finished up crawling under the house with the cup still in her hand. She could hear bullets hitting the house as it was being strafed and said she had never been so frightened in her life. If she was reluctant to leave before, they had no trouble getting rid of her after that.

We waited, wondering what we would find when we did return. Stories were already told of the looting and destruction that were going on. We could accept the enemy damage, but it really hurt to think that our army officers had failed to safeguard and protect our homes. Indeed, it seemed it was the Australians themselves who were responsible for much of the loss and damage in Darwin.

Jack Jones, a friend from Darwin, came to stay with us in Crystal Brook for a few days after his wife died. They had lived in Pine Creek where Mrs Jones had been our much-loved bush nurse. By 1941, she was in charge of the Channel Island leper hospital and was one of the last to leave in the evacuation of Darwin. One night, while we were in the dining room, an Australian air force pilot at a nearby table was bragging a bit for the benefit of the people in the room. He said: 'You know what they call us — the blue orchids.' And Jack in a disgusted voice replied, 'Well, where I come from mate, they call you the daffodils!'

It was well known that during the main Japanese bombing raid on Darwin the RAAF were told to leave the air force camp and go south into the scrub to safety. They left planes on the ground, and abandoned Darwin without any attempt at defence. Men scattered everywhere. We heard that some even made it to Adelaide. In Darwin they were known as the gutless wonders, who even failed to help after the bombing. In fairness to the RAAF personnel, there was nothing they could do to help defend Darwin. They were only following orders to leave and go into the bush. As they were not told how far into the bush to go, who could blame them?

Some of the army lads told of packing the belongings left behind by evacuees, under the orders of their officers, and taking them to their quarters. And this story was true in my case. I had bought a record player just before we were evacuated and when Ossie Jensen at whose shop I had purchased it was visiting us in Crystal Brook, he told me he had heard an army lieutenant had taken it. He was so disgusted he took it on himself to call at this officer's home in Adelaide, on the pretence of inspecting the unit. The woman said her husband had given it to her for a birthday present. Ossie checked the serial number and was certain it was mine. He felt so enraged he wrote to the officer, who returned it — after he realised Ossie was prepared to produce proof that it was mine — and he wasn't too happy about it. He had the hide to ask me to pay for the tubes he'd had replaced.

Joe had had a much more ironic experience. He had planted a stock of grog in one of our buildings in Darwin. I suspect there may have been a bit of card-playing and sly-grogging going on down there. After the bombing, he raced in from nearby Winnellie, where he was working, to check his hoard, only to find that in an incredibly short time, three hundred cases of his precious beer had been knocked off. Talk about cry over spilt grog! In all probability he would have given it away, but it was the indignity of being plundered that riled him.

None of our family really settled down at Crystal Brook, despite our efforts to make the place as much of a home away from home as possible and even after Joe joined us there. The little ones couldn't understand why in winter, they could only stay indoors and press their noses to the window pane when it was raining, instead of peeling off their duds and sitting under the gutter pipes for a soaking or running around flapping their arms to cool off. They hated getting up on winter mornings, but loved the log fires at night. It was a time for reading and telling stories, when we sat around and sewed.

My parents both helped in the hotel. Our head barman in his dark suit and bow tie, always looked more like the publican than Joe or Dad. Mum helped in the bar, and she and I had stints doing out the guest rooms on staff days off and on holidays.

On the weekends, when we had an influx of American air force boys from Port Pirie, the rooms would always be full and the town would come alive, with a dance or a picnic. They were very nice lads, always well-behaved, who seemed to be homesick and attracted to the family feel of our hotel.

The only time the children ever came into the hotel was at meal times, when Beatrice brought them over to the dining room. We often took them to Port Broughton on Sundays for a picnic, where the men did a little fishing and the children enjoyed the beach and seagulls.

The children went to school, and made friends. Marlene got what my mother called growing pains, but the doctor thought it may have been rheumatic fever, so she missed a lot of school. Warren and his very best friend rode their little three-wheelers up and down the street, and were coached — behind my back — in swear words by the local barber during his slack periods.

While in Crystal Brook we had two more additions to our family, Glenn, who was such a beautiful child with his curly blond hair that he was often mistaken for a little girl and Leonie, also a blonde. She was a shy little girl and after three sons in a row, someone for the men to spoil.

We caught up with the old fun and games when our Darwin friends called in to see us. Like the time Joe put a dead rabbit in the chamber pot under a Darwin lady's bed. A lot of commercial travellers went into shock, when they were awakened at four o'clock in the morning by a terrible scream, followed by, 'You rotten b....., Bogger Young!'

Towards the end of 1944, there were rumours and expectations of the war's end and we waited in constant anticipation of the official announcement. We stayed at Crystal Brook right up to D-Day, when we were finally told we could go home. What a joyous relief it was to be able to throw away our ration cards and shake the dust of South Australia off our feet. None of us was sorry to leave and, in the initial excitement of heading back to the Territory again, we forgot our apprehension about what we would find on our return after four years of forced absence.

· IX ·

1945–1952: STARTING AGAIN

WE HAD A CAR, but the motor blew up the morning we were to leave, so we had to leave it behind. We also had a diesel truck. On the back of this, we loaded a boat which Joe had filled with all the grog we could get our hands on. Joe had it made to his own specifications, with the intention of using it for fishing in Darwin. It was aluminium, with sealed chambers — which he said would make it unsinkable — and room for an internal engine, so it provided plenty of cargo space. We had realised that liquor would be hard to come by in the north, and the boatful would give Mum and Dad enough stock to reopen the Pine Creek Hotel.

With our few belongings, five small children, and a purseful of rail tickets, we set off. We put the truck on the train and travelled on the Ghan to Alice Springs.

It was a rotten ride. There were no sleeping cars, so we had to sit on wooden seats running along the length of the carriage. Imagine the eleven of us squeezed in with bedding, food, babies' bottles, nappies (no disposables in those days!). To make extra room for us, and to escape the chaos, Joe set up a game of cards in another part of the train. Trying to sleep on a wooden seat and cope with the heat was bad enough, but breastfeeding a baby as well was near impossible and Glenn, who was two, refused to give up his bottle, and wouldn't eat. To this day, I still don't know how we managed. The nightmare trip took two and a half days.

We were very grateful to leave the train at Alice Springs. We off-loaded the truck and rigged a cover over the back of it to make a cool and shady place for the children to sit and sleep in as we travelled.

The old diesel truck was slow and hot, and we were very crowded. It was the dry season, so we travelled as far as we could make it each day, and camped at night by the side of the road. Only a few days after leaving Alice, we broke down and one of the men had to get a lift back for a spare part. It was one of the hardest times of the trip — sitting in the shade of the truck or under a nearby tree, not knowing how long it would take to fix the truck and trying to keep the children occupied. Little Leonie felt the heat, and most of the time I had sat her in a big black iron boiler filled with water, with a green fly net over her head. Glenn fared a little better: he could move about and had Beatrice's undivided attention. It was a couple of days later, that finally, with immense relief, we started moving north again.

It was a bit nostalgic for the Dowling family, travelling up the road we had all explored together in 1929. Now, nearly twenty years later, the country looked much the same, except for the visible signs of war: the road had been rebuilt and a single lane of bitumen laid on it, which made our travelling much easier and there were fuel dumps at intervals — groups of forty-four gallon drums — and evidence of deserted army encampments. As we got further into the Territory we passed a number of airstrips which had been laid by Joe with his plant, before the government had acquired his equipment. It was a very common sight to see signs at the end of the airstrip runways saying: 'Is your IFF turned on?' which meant, Identification, friend or foe. There was one on the road before Katherine which reminded the army-truck jockeys not to belt down the bitumen: 'Katherine is no lady!'

Between Adelaide River and Darwin there were drums set in circles, packed with dirt, forming walls to serve as small gun turrets. Trees covered with miles of camouflage net made hiding places for planes near the airstrips. We saw old army camps, with toilet blocks made of drums, with chimneys sticking up the back. Once they would have had a hessian wall for privacy and now they looked very strange indeed.

We were all so intent on the journey itself, and the relief we felt as we got nearer our old haunts, that we didn't think too much about what we might find when we finally got there. We all planned to stop at Pine Creek, and rest at the hotel, and help Mum and Dad get the business going before heading on to Darwin. After nearly three weeks of travelling, our spirits lifted as the familiar hills of Pine Creek came into view. We were home at last.

Nothing could have prepared us for what we found. The hotel, which we had left intact, was a derelict wreck. Everything inside had been removed, the garden had died, and even the interior walls had been stripped. The army had used it as a recreation hall.

We were all completely stunned. We got out of the truck and stood there in shock and disbelief. Tears came to my mother's eyes as she looked at her old home. It must have nearly broken my parents' hearts. A great part of their lives had gone into making the hotel into a cheerful and comfortable home, as well as one of the best pubs in the Territory. Now, at an age when they should have been able to rest a little, they had to start all over again.

After the initial shock, we gathered ourselves together, and did what we always did in the face of disaster. Being battlers, we put our camp bedding down, lit a fire and worked out what to do first. There was no doubt about the general course of action. We would immediately start on the hard work of repairing the building and re-establishing our happy old bush pub.

My brother Jim had rejoined us after leaving his wartime job with the railways and he and Joe set to helping Dad rebuild. They worked very hard, I remember, scrounging iron from here and there and in a short time the building was on its way back to reasonable shape. There were few kitchen facilities, no cutlery, linen or furniture — all Mum and Dad's personal belongings had gone and were never recovered.

Mum and I set up a makeshift kitchen, and ordered our basic supplies to be sent down on the train from Darwin. Beatrice was kept busy with the five children, who were so relieved and happy to be in the bush, they were virtually unaware of the setbacks we had to face. Dad did his best with the bar and we were glad we had struggled back with the load of liquor. At least we had something for the regular customers, who were grateful that the hotel was once again alive and 'well'.

The men were surprised to find that the army canteen had doled out a ration of a few bottles of beer to each adult person. As Mum, Beatrice and I were non-drinkers, and as our names had been on the list, there was a stockpile which helped to keep the boys happy while they were building.

It took a long time to get back to anything like normal, of course. Mum could afford to buy only minimal supplies of bedding and utensils, so she very gradually built up her inventory. She and Dad worked long days, as they could not pay help at first. Jim stayed with them to help get things going again, and when we felt we had done as much as we could, Joe and I packed up our family again and set out for Darwin, to get our own affairs in order.

•

When we arrived, I knew just how my mother had felt at Pine Creek. Our beautiful house had been stripped bare. A temporary wooden structure had been built on to the main house, out over the wide concrete strip which Joe had carefully laid to keep the ants out of the building. The posts were set in the ground and now the building was so riddled with white ants it was unsafe to live in. I stood there with a numb, helpless feeling at the loss of all our family possessions. Once again we were reduced to a makeshift existence.

The house which we had built for my parents' retirement had been used as a communications centre. It too was now empty, except for office benches set up along the wall in the kitchen area. The roof was riddled with bullet holes where it had been strafed during the raids.

We had to start from scratch. After the evacuation, we had been given a little compensation money by the government, which had helped us buy the hotel at Crystal Brook. A law was made during the war which prohibited the resale of any business for more than the purchase price, so we only got out of Crystal Brook what we had paid for it — not a huge amount. This was all we had.

But Joe was always a battler too, and it wasn't long before he was on his feet again and back into business in Darwin. Every bit of money he could make with his own hard labour he would reinvest. We fixed up my parents' house as best we could and made a home of it, despite having no furniture other than our camp bedding and cooking gear. There was no stove, so we set up a fire outside, until we could put the kitchen back together again.

Joe had his own way of making up for the lack of real compensation for the loss of our property. He scrounged around among the abandoned army gear, and found iron beds, a few cupboards, an old fuel stove, some tubs for me to use for washing, and a few lengths of unbleached calico on to which I sewed strips of bright gingham, to make curtains. The children quickly became happy and settled, many of our old friends were returning to Darwin and putting their houses back in order, and we felt pleased to be there. Our sense of loss and disappointment was replaced with one of new hope and the challenge of purposeful rebuilding.

•

AFTER THE WAR, a lot of the army's surplus gear was sold in lots at auction. There were some very good buys, if you were lucky enough to have the money. Most of the bargains went interstate, bought by southern businessmen who had solid assets and could afford to buy. Darwin people who had lost everything didn't have the cash to compete for such things as the heavy machinery, which had been requisitioned from them by the government and was now being resold. That's what happened to Joe's original roadmaking plant. Once this sort of equipment went south it meant we had to pay a great deal more later on to acquire new machinery from the Southern states. This really set the Territory back for quite some time.

Joe put together as much cash as he could, and tried to buy more plant. The auctioned lots could contain anything from Jeep engines to empty drums or prefabricated outhouses. One lot that he bought contained an item listed as a thunder box. When a chap came up and asked Joe if he would sell it, he replied, 'I don't know what it is, let's have a look first.' He was amused to find it was a toilet — a forty-four gallon drum with a hole cut in one end and a wooden seat with lid to fit. The army called them thunder boxes or flaming furies — the last because once a day oil was poured into the drums and set alight. If you were a bit slow on the job it was easy to finish up with singed eyelashes and possibly a crew-cut as well!

Joe could see so many clean forty-four gallon drums of no use to anyone lying around rusting in the bush, that he went to see one of the oil companies and put a proposition to them. They were in need of drums, and were very pleased with the deal: he gave them a price for the drums on the wharf, as he delivered. He approached people whom he knew had bought lots at the auctions consisting in part of empty drums, and offered them a price for any that were in good condition. Cash down, and a shake of the hand sealed the deal. All went well until others started to see it was quite a good moneymaker, and moved in. Someone laid a complaint against Joe, and charged him with stealing a thousand drums.

All our drums were confiscated, taken to the police station and impounded. The court case which followed went on for almost twelve months. In the first hearing, Joe was found guilty, and given a nine-month prison sentence. He requested a retrial. This time he flew in a QC from Adelaide to handle his case — a very expensive course of action, but the only one we could see open to us. When the case finally ended, Judge Wells said that the thirty-six pages of deposition on the trial was the longest in Northern Territory history. He gave a 'Not Guilty' verdict in Joe's favour, and ordered that the thousand drums had to stay in the police yard for two years, as 'a monument to the inefficiency of the Northern Territory Police Force'.

If you ever heard the sound of drums rolling across the road and heading for the cliffs on the Lameroos Beach at night, you could bet your boots that someone had pulled the chocks away. And you couldn't blame Joe, because inevitably on these occasions he would be in a pub drinking, where everyone could see him! No doubt some of the local wags — who would have been sent out to deal with the chocks on Joe's behalf — profited from the exercise. So we were all happy except for the police boys who had to retrieve the wayward drums, and restack and chock them again.

The drum case cost Joe a lot of money and there was more trouble in store for us. Joe was a strong man and always came up fighting, but we took one hard knock after another at this time in our lives.

•

EARLY IN 1949 we lost a son, our sixth child. He was born in the Darwin Hospital. One day, I was holding the beautiful, seemingly healthy little bundle in my arms, and the next he seemed to be having breathing problems. They put him in an oxygen tent, but he still struggled with his breathing and a minister was called in to christen him. We found out then he had a congenital heart condition and we only had him with us for ten days. Ten days, ten weeks, ten years, whatever — the loss is just the same and none the less deep. How do you explain this grief? I turned my face to the wall and cried myself dry. For a while I forgot that others were grieving with me, in time I realised I was not alone and that I had a family who needed me. Life went on.

We tried our best to keep a happy atmosphere in the house for the children and, as we had done before the war, we made a habit of going to the beach for picnics on the weekends. One of our best buys from the army auctions, was an American army duck. It was a large amphibious vehicle, with a deep timber tray in the middle where I could rig up shelter for the babies to play and sleep, and where I could also sit and fish, knowing they were safe. We would load the duck up at the house and drive it down to the sea and away for a day's fishing. Often, if we missed the tide, we would get bogged trying to get out, and would have to wait for the tide to turn. The duck as we all called it, gave us many happy outings.

Once, we went to Ossie Jensen's place across the harbour, to see Bill Harney, the writer — an old friend of many years. An Aboriginal friend saw us come out of the water, and yelled to Bill, 'Boss, that one duck, him bin cumminup!'

Bill yelled back, 'Don't be bloody silly, there's no ducks around here!'

The fellow insisted: 'Duck him bin cumminup orright!'

And, it did, with us in it and a good catch of fish. We sat around the fire with Bill, and ate fish and had a wonderful evening. Bill was a great character and story teller who could entertain for hours with his amusing and interesting yarns.

Bill was a real bushman. He believed the best way to keep the mozzies at bay was to put mud over your body and let it dry there. It formed a kind of mud suit of armour against the attacking insects. I had recently purchased one of Bill's books for the children to give to Joe for his birthday. I explained to them that it was written by our friend Bill, but it was very hard for me to convince Marlene that this muddy man in shorts, who was filleting the fish, was really the same man that had written the book!

After the loss of the baby, the doctor had said to me 'Go home and have another baby', and Sandra, our seventh child, was born almost a year to the day later.

During 1949, when I was pregnant with Sandra, Joe had his second big business disaster. He had purchased a lot of equipment from the army which had been abandoned by the RAAF on the Truscott airstrip, in the north of Western Australia. The best way of getting the machinery over to Darwin was by boat, so Joe hired a barge-type vessel. He told me that it was without an engine, so he had paid the barge owner five hundred pounds, in advance, to enable him to purchase the right engine to do the job.

Joe put his best diesel mechanic, George Axam, to work installing the engine on the barge. The *Phoenix* left Darwin in June 1949. On board were the owner and two of Joe's best men, George Axam and David Cullen and George's mate, his dog. They took also Joe's truck and lighting plant, welding gear and other equipment which they thought would be useful for loading the gear for the return trip.

They had an uneventful trip across, and when

they got there they kept in touch from Truscott by radio phone. When the load was ready, they sent word to Joe that they were leaving. Unfortunately, they failed to tell him that without his approval, a large number of forty-four gallon drums of highly explosive gasoline had also been taken on board. Joe would never have consented to this had he known about it. As he had paid for the trip, nothing else should have gone on to the barge and that is why the men had not told him about it. Later we heard that it was a private deal made by the owner of the barge and one of his Darwin friends.

Perhaps George didn't tell Joe because he didn't want to cause any trouble. Whatever the reason, the barge left Truscott and was never seen again.

When they had not shown up after some time Joe became alarmed. Everything possible was done: the navy and air force sent out searchers and Joe hired private planes to fly every possible route they might have taken, looking for wreckage, floating drums, oil slicks — anything. The beaches were searched for months afterwards, but no sign of the men, the cargo, or the barge was ever sighted. The fate of the *Phoenix* and her crew was a mystery.

The drum case was a fight, Joe could handle that. But this was a personal tragedy, and for a long time he was a broken man. He had lost his men and his friends, and that affected him very deeply. He had also lost a great deal of money in equipment for which there was no insurance, and the truck and other equipment which had enabled him to take out the road contracts. He picked up the pieces and carried on, but I felt that he never had quite the same old spirit afterwards. It slowed him down, and like all tragedies in life, deep down it stayed with him.

•

BY 1950, Mum and Dad had got the Pine Creek Hotel back onto its feet again, and when the Parap Hotel in

Darwin came up for sale, they decided to buy it and move where they would be closer to us. The Parap Hotel was about two and a half miles out of the centre of Darwin, and it serviced the people of the railway yards and civil airstrip, and scattered settlers. They leased out the Pine Creek Hotel.

By this time, Jim had married a lovely girl who had come up to Pine Creek after the war and they too came back to Darwin and worked with my parents at the Parap Hotel. Mum, Dad, Jim, Dot and their babies often joined us on our Sunday picnics. I'd spend all Friday cooking and all Saturday packing for the Sunday outing with five lively children. We had some of our happiest and most memorable days on those occasions.

Joe had got together a truck and a loader — enough plant to be able to get some roadmaking work again. He even went down as far as Tennant Creek, where he put in a dam for the town water supply. He was often away on these jobs, and when he was in Darwin we didn't see a lot of him. He was not the type to play much with the children — but they knew he was about. Although he was very strict, I can't remember him ever lifting his hand to them. His word was law, and the children respected that, and they loved him. He always tried to get home in time to sit down to have a meal with us, and would set aside a day as often as possible for a family outing.

In 1952, our youngest daughter arrived. Susanne was dark-haired and dark-eyed like Warren, and Joe called her his 'little black-eyed Sue'. She was such a sweet child, she was thoroughly spoilt by all of us.

One of my best friends at this time was Poppy Secrett. She was my neighbour and we had children the same age. We became great friends; our children grew up together and were like brothers and sisters to each other. She was responsible for me coming out of my shell. She nominated me for committees and pushed me into public speaking, and she would call around and insist that I join in social activities. Due to her enthusiasm and persuasiveness I found myself gaining a confidence in public which I had never had before. I became active in organising functions, and thoroughly enjoyed playing a role outside the house after being so tied down to house and children and the domestic routine since my marriage. I have a lot to thank Poppy for. She was amongst those who were reluctantly evacuated in 1942, refusing to be separated from her husband. She actually made her way back as far as Dunmarra, to the dismay of the army!

· X ·

1952–1959: KATHERINE

IN 1950, the Commercial Hotel (later renamed The Crossways), came up for sale in Katherine. Joe and I discussed it and decided we should go down to Katherine to inspect it. We drove down, with the intention of staying the night and possibly talking the deal over while we were there.

Katherine is a 'station' town, the centre of some of the richest cattle grazing country in the Territory and the main town between Darwin and Alice Springs. When we lived there in the 1950s the population was about 2000 people.

The hotel was small and very run-down. The building appeared to have grown piecemeal, room by room. It was made of corrugated iron, with cement floors; there was no lining on the walls, no fans, rough old furniture and the barest essentials for the bar and kitchen. Although it was in the main street, it was a rough old bush pub. Our night spent there was a disaster. It had been a roasting hot day, and the place was like an oven. Someone kindly lent me a small table fan, which helped, but big grey cattle ticks crawled over the cement floor and up the walls, and the bed sank hopelessly in the middle. This was nothing, however, to the sound effects I was treated to through the night.

The licensee had had a 'blue' with his wife, and had been missing for some time. She spotted him getting out of a car driven by a girl, but by the time she had caught up with him, he had jumped into bed, fully clothed, pulled the sheet up under his chin and was doing a good imitation of a man who was fast asleep.

'You bastard!' she yelled, for everyone within a mile to hear, as she ripped the sheet off and hit him squarely between the eyes with the stiletto heel of one of her shoes.

He let out a yell and tried to grab her, but she was fleet of foot and had a head start. Grabbing a lump of wood along the way, she kept lashing out at him and finally got clear and hid behind the empty bottle crates in the back yard.

He was worse than ten tom cats, prowling around half the night with his torch telling the 'bitch' what he was going to do when he found her.

Needless to say, I got very little sleep, and was not impressed by the hotel! I left Joe to work things out for himself, and went back to Darwin. He decided to buy it and stayed there to see through the purchase and get the place running.

During the few months when I went back to Darwin before returning to Katherine, I believe Joe had a great time. He liked drinking and playing up with his mates, and from what I heard there had been plenty of that going on while I wasn't there. According to one story, which I read much later in a journalist's account of the Commercial Hotel, Joe lost the lease for a time when he gambled it on the outcome of a game of darts! I can well believe it — he was quite capable of making such a bet.

Joe finally leased the hotel to a young couple, who did a good job until the wife got appendicitis and died from blood poisoning. There were still twelve months of the lease to go, and Joe gave it to a couple I did not consider suitable. The place was still dilapidated, so when that year was up, I decided to take over the running of the hotel myself. Susanne was just two years old but I felt I should return to work to hold things together. We were not hard up, but I couldn't bear to watch the business go downhill.

When I went back to Katherine in 1953, I didn't really know anyone, but in the Territory it didn't take long to meet the locals. I couldn't help thinking how different it was from the closed snobbery of Crystal Brook, in South Australia, where the women pointedly had made my mother and me feel like second-class citizens. Here, there was no stigma attached to a hotel. I was treated as a lady and with great friendliness by the Katherine women, who made a point of calling in to say hello and invited me to join in their activities. Our family were very quickly made to feel at home.

Joe was still doing contract roadmaking, but on a much smaller scale since the *Phoenix* disaster. He lived out wherever the work was, and came back to work at the hotel in between jobs.

Little dark-eyed Susanne was the only one of the children not at school. She was an easy child, and there was always someone to keep an eye on her. We all lived at the hotel while I got things going. I set aside a row of bedrooms side by side, and these became our family quarters. The place was so old and run-down, I decided it had to be renovated. It was rebuilt in stages, while the hotel continued to function, and when it was completed we actually had an entirely new hotel.

The new-look Commercial had a large easy-to-manage bar, with good electric refrigeration; a small ladies lounge, or saloon bar; a beer garden; a decent kitchen and dining room, and good accommodation. When it was completed it looked great, and we were very proud of it.

Later we installed a stage at the bottom of the beer garden and on some Saturday nights we applied for a late-night licence and had a dance. We had a piano and the old tea-chest bases, perhaps an accordion, and any other instrument around at the time. It was always fun and the locals really enjoyed themselves. On Saturday mornings the mums did the weekly shopping while the dads relaxed in the bar! Lunch time found parcels of groceries stacked here and there, sandwiches and pies mixed with beer glasses and babies' milk bottles on the tables, with the fathers ducking over to the (illegal) bookmaker for a bet on the horses. It was always free raspberry drink for the kids at the Commercial. My mother always said that the kids of today are the potential customers of tomorrow, and it really proved to be true. Today I am serving the children of those times, and in some cases, their children too.

Mind you when the Katherine women held progressive dinners for one of their fund-raising functions, the hostesses had to hide from me the fancy glasses 'borrowed' from the hotel and purchased during a period when I went a bit superior and attempted to up-grade the ladies lounge!

One night a local chap committed suicide during a progressive dinner. The police sergeant and his wife were enjoying themselves, and commented as they left that they thought the unfortunate man 'was pretty thoughtless not only to cut his throat, but also to jump into an overhead tank of water — in the middle of the night, and in the rain too!'

For a time we had trouble with the more aggressive alcoholics waylaying our older wine drinkers on their way home at night and taking their precious bottles of plonk. On his way home one night, one of these old blokes came face to face with a big figure which loomed up in front of him. 'Step aside you bastard!' he roared. When the bastard refused to move he 'fitted' him with his fist, only to finish up with a broken hand full of cuts. He had punched a horse fair in the mouth!

The Katherine locals did play a bit rough at times, but it was only a way of letting off steam. We had some great fist fights, some in the bar but usually outside. I used to say to them, 'If you want to fight, go out on the flat where you won't hurt yourself!' I have seen heads pushed through the fibro-cement walls of the hotel and horses ridden into the bar. One lad was so proud of his American saddle, he couldn't be parted with it, he either brought his horse in with him, or carried his saddle over his shoulder and dumped it on the bar where he could keep an eye on it. I wouldn't mind a quid either, for every time a truck with rotten brakes came through the wall of the Commercial, to finish up in the bar. It was all in a day's work.

When the Redex car trials passed through Katherine, we all turned out to see them go down in the bulldust. Some of the enterprising locals with tractors earned quite a bit pulling them out. The famous radio personality, Jack Davey, was among the drivers and he came round to the hotel for a few drinks. He wrote 'Hi, ho Mayse' and signed his name across my bar book, and left us proud to have met him.

The bushman is a great prankster, and we had lots of fun. I can remember when one lady tourist went into the 'Ladies', only to find a big red kangaroo (dead, of course), sitting on the toilet seat. You could have heard her yell as far as Mataranka, seventy-four miles away!

To see a man come into the bar with a python snake wrapped around his middle was an everyday happening, but I never really got used to watching a scaly head slide out around a collar, or from under a shirt to prowl along the bar counter.

Marlene always said the most awful thing she could remember was watching, wide-eyed, as her father and his friends dropped little frogs into the open mouth of one of their mates who was sleeping it off. Some jumped out, but when the poor bloke smacked his lips and rolled over, he gulped and swallowed at least one.

Although I had the hotel running smoothly, Joe was restless and decided to turn to cattle work instead of mining or roadmaking. He bought Moroak Station, out between Mataranka and the Elsey Station, but he held on to his plant and other investments.

He tried hard to make a go of it — but you need experience to be a good cattle man, and Joe didn't have that background. He wasn't really a cattle man at heart; he had done it because of the dissatisfaction which he always seemed to carry with him after the *Phoenix* accident. I stayed at the hotel to keep our finances in shape, so it meant that we never had a chance of trying to battle it out together on the station. In the end, he said that he couldn't be three places at once and he sold Moroak. He wasn't getting any younger either, and it was a bit too far down the track for an old dog to try to learn new tricks.

However, when it came to a fight, Joe could still hold his own with the young dogs in Katherine. One of the local larrikins, renowned as a lightweight champion, was banging on the door one day and Joe said, 'Look mate, do that again and I'll have to thump you!'

The young bloke looked Joe up and down and said, 'There's only two things stopping you, old chap: one, you're too bloody old, and two, you can't fight!' Joe said: 'Step around the back, and we'll see how bloody old I am!' They did just that, and Joe left him flat-out on his back in the dirt. (To give the fellow his due, he did apologise later, and they went and had a few drinks to their renewed friendship.)

When Joe came back to Katherine after selling up at Moroak, we bought the Bovril company site (now a caravan park), just out of town, on the Victoria Highway. It had two houses on it and we moved into the largest one, which we called the big white house.

It was wonderful for us to have our own private family home. We had plenty of land, a couple of horses, chooks, a dog, not to mention my big brood of growing kids, their friends and a lovely girl, Pauline Scott, who kept house for me. Most of the kids in Katherine came to play at Aunty Mayse's place. I was happy because I knew where my children were, and I think the other mothers were happy too.

I had a lovely rose garden which was quite something in Katherine in those days as there weren't many elaborate gardens. There was a big lawn, and a lily pond in the front garden, which every dog would flop into just to cool off, and which every passing horse used as a drinking trough. Eventually I had to put a fence around the garden, not just to keep the horses and dogs out, but the wild donkeys as well. Those little darlings would frighten the life out of us when they brayed outside the window at night!

Show week, in July, was always the big social event of the year in Katherine. All the people from the stations, the bosses, the managers, the wives, the children, the ringers, and all who could get away came to town, to set up camp on the showground, and to spend a week of talking, drinking, catching up with each other and with the year's gossip.

The first day was always a time of great excitement, as cars full of people with their supplies and swags and trucks loaded with horses drove in, churning up the red dust. Temporary yards were made for the horses, and tarpaulins and tucker wagons set up to make the base camp for each station, all around the showground. It was all happy yells, smiles and waves, as old friends greeted each other and kids and dogs raced around in excitement. By the end of the week, it was amusing to notice that the same faces were starting to bite the bit to get going home again. By then, everyone and everything was covered with dust, the kids, dogs and some of the men were reliving old feuds, and there was evidence of quite a few hangovers. The station people reckoned they lived hard and played hard, and after a week's hard play they had usually had their fill of their annual socialising. On the last day the women too were packing up, anxious to get everyone off to the peace and quiet of their isolated stations.

A race meeting was included in show week events. Before one of these occasions, one of the local ladies challenged me to a race, unfortunately within earshot of the fellows in the bar. I thought she meant a foot race, and replied cheekily, 'I'd race you any old day!'

The fellows took up the idea with great gusto and made all the arrangements. I later found out that it was the ladies' bracelet she was referring to — on horseback.

When it was time for the event, the all-male race committee refused to recognise it officially, because the jockeys were 'amateur women riders', and adjourned to the bar for the duration, to make their protest more pointed.

However, the rest of the crowd were good sports, and had been waiting for the event enthusiastically — which was more than I could say for myself. But by then, I couldn't pull out!

One of the locals lent me a decent horse, and I rode around to the starting post with the clerk of the course. I told him that I was only doing this to make it look good, and that I had no intention of actually running.

He said: Be a sport, there are only four of you in the race! So I shortened the reins, tried to look like a jockey and off I went.

I won. My horse was a mile in front and 'galloping easy', when I flew past the post. Then still galloping easy, it left the track — as it had done after its previous races — and headed back to the horse yards, leaping over fallen logs, and antbeds. This was a bit too much for me, I knew that I couldn't stay on much longer, so I slipped my feet out of the stirrups and hit the dust voluntarily.

We all got a bit of a fright, the horse included. I had a few lumps and bumps, a black and blue cheek, and I limped very badly around the bar for the next few days. There were a lot of laughs at my expense, and plenty of cheek from the customers at the Commercial for a while afterwards. There was no money on it, but as it turned out, I paid!

•

BY 1953 MY FAMILY was growing up. Marlene was married and had two little girls. They all came back to live with me in the big white house. Then Russell, who had stayed in Darwin to train as a diesel mechanic, came back because he was homesick, and Warren, who also had been living in Darwin with my mother to finish his secondary schooling, decided against academic life and got a job as a stockman on Manballoo, a Vestey's Station out of Katherine.

Secondary schooling was always a problem in the bush. Leonie, Sandra and Susanne were all happy at school in Katherine. Glenn went to the Inland Mission school in Darwin, but would hitch a ride whenever he felt inclined. The teachers got a bit tired of this exercise, and so did I. So I sent him to Alice Springs to board. This turned out to be as heartbreaking for him as it was for me, so I let him come home after the first year. He was about fifteen.

On Christmas Eve 1954, the local ladies decided to hold a 'Carols by Candlelight' in Katherine. We put our decorated Christmas tree in a forty-four gallon drum cut in half and filled with sand. We handed out candles, with little white cardboard holders, to the children and to anyone else who was present. The old wind-up gramophone played a selection of Christmas carols and we all sang our hearts out. I wasn't surprised to see several of my old alcoholic friends, hats in hands, singing too, and it touched me deeply to see the younger station boys, some of whom were far from home, singing along, unashamed of the tears running down their cheeks.

•

IN 1957 WE HAD a big flood in Katherine. The usual drop to the river level at the railway bridge is sixty feet; when the flood came, the waters were just three inches below the bridge. That was a lot of water! The river finally broke its banks at the back of the town. Had it risen over the bridge, it's doubtful that much of Katherine would still stand today.

Fortunately for me, the Commercial Hotel was still on dry ground but the Katherine Hotel, further up the street, was flooded. The customers there could sit on their bar stools drinking and wash their own glasses without moving. One of our visiting clergymen said that he sat on a stool in the bar praying for the rain to stop. I think he was jesting, as it was popularly considered a pretty good place to be at the time!

As the rain kept falling and the river kept rising, many of my friends decided that the big white house — which was high up on stilts, was the safest place to be. One night, I had fifty extra mouths to feed and bodies to bed down — men, women and children.

We had a very merry evening singing and telling stories, and left the weather to do its worst. Next morning, it was a different story. The water was up to the top step — over nine feet deep across the garden. We were marooned. Bags of chaff and bales of hay floated around with chooks and snakes as passengers. Everyone who could swim was jumping off the veranda and having great fun.

We pushed all the vehicles we could reach up to higher ground, led the horses to safety through the water, and rowboats appeared to evacuate the women, kids, and non-swimmers. We all finished up at the Commercial Hotel, which was still one of the driest places in town. The men kindly went back to the white house, to check things. They would reappear carrying chickens and we ate roast chook and chook cooked any other way we could think of for days. It wasn't until later that I found out I had been enjoying my own poultry!

●

FOR ME, THE WORST aspect of being in Katherine was that I was so far away from my parents. We had always been such good friends. Mum and Dad were so tied down, running the Parap Hotel in Darwin, that it was impossible for them to get down to Katherine. Hard work was a habit with them, they rarely took holidays. I managed to get up to Darwin to visit them now and again, and I was very appreciative on the occasions when Mum would give me a couple of hundred pounds and send me out shopping for a new frock and special things for the children.

Not long after the flood my father died. The doctor said he was just worn out from hard work. He worked at the Parap Hotel right up until the end. Four months later, my mother also passed away. She was only sixty.

I loved both my parents very much, and had shared so much with them over the years; they had always been a great support to me. The loss of my mother, so soon after my father, hit me like a great blow. I was suddenly cut off from them both forever and experienced the terrible realisation that they were no longer there. I had always had a very special relationship with my mother and even today, some thirty years later, I find myself getting tearful think-ing of her.

Joe and I were concerned about the boys' future, so when Birrindudu Station was put up for sale by ballot, Joe successfully applied on their behalf. It was a beautiful cattle station — approximately 1500 square miles, situated on the edge of The Great Sandy Desert, next to Nicholson and Hooker Stations, over near the Western Australia/Northern Territory border.

Unfortunately our boys were far too young and inexperienced to handle such a large property. They had a manager for a while, who worked with them, but he didn't provide them with enough of the train-ing and guidance they needed. Joe went out there with them when he could, but he really wasn't much help, as his only previous experience with cattle was at Moroak. I could only stay behind the bar and earn money at the hotel to keep them going, hoping they would eventually get on their feet.

It was a worrying time for me, but I did what I have always done when things are looking down — kept myself working and held the family together, hoping that somehow this would get us through.

In 1958 we sold the Commercial Hotel to the Swan Brewery. My mother had left the Pine Creek Hotel to me in her will. The Parap in Darwin went to my brother Jim.

I wanted to go back to Pine Creek to run our hotel, which had deteriorated badly, and needed a lot of work to bring it back to scratch. I sent Russell up to Pine Creek to mind it temporarily, and I had a quiet time at the white house — if being mother and grandmother to a house full of children can be called quiet — until we were ready to move the whole family up to Pine Creek the following year.

Katherine had been a good town to live in, and we kept the lovely big white house, with the intention that we would be coming back one day. Even though I had been so busy managing the hotel and running our home, I had found time to be part of the many community activities in Katherine.

Different women's committees worked hard, and I had been actively involved in many of these including the Parents' and Citizens' Association, the Country Women's Association and the Red Cross.

I was made President of the local Red Cross Society, and had a marvellous group of workers behind me. We raised money and built the first retirement village for the elderly citizens of Katherine. We called it the old men's home, probably because there were no old women around who were homeless! These old chaps were old bushies and stockmen, who didn't have families. When it was officially opened by the Northern Territory Administrator and his wife, it was a grand affair for Katherine. The boy scouts formed a guard of honour, and we held a garden party on the lawns at the big white house.

Being President of the Red Cross meant I officiated at all the VIP visits to Katherine, meeting the sirs, and ladies, the honourables and importances. When Joe and I were invited to meet HRH Prince Philip at Government House in Darwin, I thought, 'This is a far cry from the barefoot bush girl and the little tent beside the railway line at Maranboy!'

· XI ·

1959–1963: INTO MY MOTHER'S SHOES

'YOU WILL NEVER be as great a lady as your mother,' some of the old timers said when I went back to take over the Pine Creek Hotel, but despite this warning, I found that her shoes fitted me very well. I soon became friend, mother confessor and banker — as there was no bank in town — to most of Pine Creek. The hotel was in effect the local hall, church, office for men doing business, meeting place, home away from home and, occasionally, dog house.

Pine Creek could be called little, but never sleepy. The place was always buzzing with the news and business of the goldmines and the station people for a hundred or so miles around, and the hotel was the centre of it. I enjoyed being back there again.

By 1958, the original hotel building was on the old side. Actually we were told it could be condemned as the hotel licensing commission were starting to take a 'skinny squint' at it. We realised the only thing to do was to build a new one.

The former main street, where the old hotel was situated, was now at the back of the town. So we purchased a site on the new road into Pine Creek. We planned the layout ourselves. After the usual turmoil of getting the land and permission to rebuild and have plans passed, the two Joes — my husband and his friend little Joe Fahey, so called because he was the shorter of the two — started putting machinery in place to dig the foundations. Work was about to begin, when someone made the discovery they had the wrong site. The two Joes took a bit of convincing before the big transfer got underway.

The new hotel looked great. It was a solid, well laid-out two-storeyed brick building, with a shady pergola in front, and a central courtyard-cum beer garden. It had good equipment and refrigeration — we had our own generator — overhead fans, green cement floors and fifteen rooms for accommodation — everything just as it should be in a first-class country hotel. Once the garden took shape, people said that as you came over the rise into the town, it looked like an oasis in the desert.

We combined the official opening of the hotel with Russell's wedding, on the same day in 1959. It was a great affair. Southern newspapers rang in to find out how I was going to accommodate all the guests, and one reporter asked if any were coming on camels! 'And would there be big nuggets of gold among the gifts?' I replied, 'We're way back ... but not that bloody way back!' In fact, after the festivities, those who could not be fitted into the hotel accommodation slept outside in their cars or in swags, and some ended up in the new rockery at the front of the hotel, where they'd fallen.

After this start with a bang, the hotel got on with its day-to-day business, and became our family home. It had its bad moments, but for the younger children growing up without television to distract them and in the safety of a small town where there was an extended family environment, meant they enjoyed a carefree life. They fished, picnicked and swam, roamed the bush and fossicked in the creek and gullies for gold or pretty stones — all the same occupations I had loved as a girl in Pine Creek. The old Chinatown rubbish dumps offered up earthenware jars, bits of china and odd trinkets which were exciting, even for us oldies.

•

MY CONTENTMENT was shattered when, without any real consultation with me, Joe sold the big white house in Katherine. Although we had moved up to Pine Creek, I was devastated. My lovely family home, into which I had put so much effort and of which the children were so fond, was gone. This was a terrible emotional blow. It hurt me very deeply, because he had cast away something thoughtlessly which had meant so much to us as a family. Also, it infuriated me that it had been one of his typical spontaneous business deals — more than likely made in the hotel bar — and he had virtually given the house away.

From then on, although Joe came back and forth to the Pine Creek Hotel, he was out most of the time with the boys on the station, and we remained distant with each other. I erected an emotional barrier for my own sake. I tried not to let the children see how difficult the situation had become. Once again, I put my efforts into the business and maintaining a sense of security for the kids.

I was good at the hotel business, and I could knuckle down and earn good money from it. Some still may consider a hotel no place for a woman, but I just followed my mother's example. The tone in the place was set by the lady behind the bar, and my hotels were always places where women felt just as much at ease as the men.

When it came to business deals and decisions, experience filled in whatever I hadn't learned from my parents and I came to clearly understand wheeling and dealing. In those days, business was still considered a man's world, and Joe would often make decisions without any discussion with me. I would feel both angry and helpless when they turned out to be bad deals, especially when it was my hard-earned money which had been lost in the exercise!

At this time, my mind turned back to my mother and many times I had a quiet weep missing her. It was she who had left the Pine Creek Hotel in my name, and who had ensured that I now had a place which was my own. I decided then, looking at my growing daughters, that I would make sure that they would have all the benefit of my experience, I would encourage them to try to have financial independence.

While I wanted them to enjoy their youthful, optimistic dreams of romance and love, I did not want them to expect that any man, no matter how right for them, would provide everything.

•

FORTUNATELY, the demanding and lively life of the hotel left little time for brooding, and feeling sorry for myself. Pine Creek was the same warm little community. Old friendships from the earlier years were picked up where they had left off, and I felt as if I had returned home. And at the hotel there were always people to be fed and looked after, and the constant bush larrikinism kept everyone's spirits up.

I always followed my mother's advice to look after your own customers. In fact, this meant if any of my regular boys had a bit too much I would put them to bed and make sure they had a feed when they woke up. There are fellows all over the Territory who still call me Mum!

Racing about the bar, I found it was easier for me to push notes, loose change, keys, and all the other bits and pieces the boys would give me to mind down the front of my frock and tuck them into my bra. The cheeky boys referred to this convenient spot as Mum's treasure chest. One night, one of the local lads was getting ready to go out on the flat for a punch-up. He took his top plate, adorned with his two front teeth, out of his mouth and asked me to mind it for him. In the excitement of the moment, it too went into the treasure chest!

When a bushman, as was the custom of the ringers, came in and threw his cheque on the counter saying 'Tell us when it cuts out, Missus', you did the right thing by him, making sure he slept off hangovers and had good meals. When the time came for him to go bush again, you sobered him up, and headed him home with a couple of bottles of rum in his saddlebag. The old crinkle bottles of Beenleigh rum were said to go ten miles to the crinkle! I never knew how it measured by horseback, but I did hear in Katherine that the nearest thing to paradise was a bottle of rum, a pannikin, and a lie down in the cool waters of the Katherine River at the low level crossing.

I often asked the stockmen, who worked so hard for a living droving cattle in the dusty hot dry season, why they didn't go south for their holidays. The answer was always the same:

'Why go to a place where you are a stranger? If you get drunk you finish up in the lock-up. If you sit outside on the street — back to the house of correction; no singing or dancing, yelling or yahooing; no bull-tossing on the bar-room floor; if your new boots hurt your feet, you tie the laces together and hang them around your neck then you are trouble; you pay through the nose for lodging, and even the girls cost more than down at Gun Alley! No, it is better to stay in your own territory.'

'The best pub in the Territory', or 'My favourite watering hole' was the way most people referred to the Pine Creek Hotel, and I'd set my boys with the best of them. Mind you, some of them would probably try to convince you that they owned a big share of the place, or paid for half the bar at least but, as you know, we breed some of the biggest liars in Australia up there, too!

•

MY THREE SONS were all stockmen out at Birrindudu Station. It worried me that they were so young, and out there on their own. But when I saw them, they made light of it, and made us all laugh with their funny stories about some of the things that had happened.

Carlien, Russell's wife, played the bagpipes, and while she lived out on the station, she would occasionally pull them out, and give them a blow. The Aboriginal girls said she had a poor old pussy cat caught in the bag, and that she was a very cruel missus, because she kept him there and made him yell by pushing him with her arm when she wanted him to cry out!

The 'bush brothers', based in Katherine, were a group of bachelor Church of England ministers, who travelled around the stations, mines, and other lonely outposts. They were a great group of men, on whom you could always rely to supply the news of local doings, who would christen your child, or lend a shoulder to cry on when needed. Brother Hamish christened Russell's son Mark, out at Birrindudu. During the visit, he decided to go for a ride with the boys. Russell said he got on the horse all right, but the animal had other ideas — he reared up in the air, and poor Brother Hamish kept going upward. The boys reckoned he landed in the soft red dirt of the stock yard, and left a perfect gingerbread man imprint!

On one occasion, Glenn drove one of the young Birrindudu lubras and her sick old grandmother back to Hooker Creek, because this was her home country, and the old woman wanted to go back there to die. Miles out of Hooker Creek, however, his car ran out of petrol; he could not persuade the women to sit and wait for help. They just walked toward Hooker Creek. Nothing was going to stop the old lady — sick as she was — getting to Hooker Creek. He heard she died peacefully soon afterwards.

Joe still had his plant working while the boys were out at Birrindudu, though not on a large scale. He would go out to the station as often as he could, taking gear and supplies. Once he was transporting a prefabricated building made of steel angle and galvanised iron to erect a new house for one of the boys. He got bogged on the way and had to unload the truck and then take it back to town for repair. By the time he got back to pick up the load and continue the trip out to Birrindudu, the house had completely disappeared. No doubt it was erected somewhere else — but we never found out where.

Another time, he loaded up one of his trucks with diesel and other gear, and sent it out with a driver to the station. After a time, when it hadn't shown up, he discovered that the driver had hijacked the truck and the load, and headed for Queensland. The truck was later found in a small town, minus its load and driver. Joe had to go two thousand or so miles to get the truck back!

While they were at Birrindudu we nearly lost Warren. There were always accidents and spills during the horse-breaking and mustering seasons, and these were accepted as everyday occurrences. However, one day while out mustering, Warren and another stockman went after the same bullock which had broken out from the mob. Being young and full of life, they made a race of it and pressed their horses into a flat gallop. The other horse had the edge on Warren, and turned the bullock, which swerved across his path and collided with his horse. Both bullock and horse fell, and kept rolling. As Warren landed on the ground, his horse rolled over him.

His mates rushed to his side, to find him unconscious. They carried him to the truck and then took him the thirty miles back into the station homestead on the rough road, before they could call for help. They were all worried, as it was obviously a very serious head injury.

It took nearly twenty-four hours after the accident happened for the flying doctor to arrive, and he was flown to Darwin Hospital. The other boys got on the pedal wireless at Birrindudu, and rang me at the hotel to tell me what had happened. I just dropped everything, got in the car, and raced to Darwin.

I can't remember how long he stayed in a coma. Each day I sat by his bedside, just watching him, not knowing whether he would live or die, or have some terrible permanent disability.

One morning, as I sat beside the bed, the young lad in the next bed said to me 'He spoke to me last night, Missus.' Looking at Warren, still unconscious, and not daring to believe him, I asked, 'What did he say?' 'Well,' the lad replied, 'he sat up, looked around and said to me, "Who are you, you mongrel bastard?" and then he went back to sleep.'

That was my son, all right! The relief was so great I felt like crying, but it was so funny I just had to laugh. It took Warren a long time to get over that spill. It didn't leave him with any permanent problems, but he didn't go back out to Birrindudu. When he was well enough he came back to Pine Creek, and helped me in the hotel for a while. Birrindudu Station finally got too much for the other two boys and Joe just sold it up and brought them back to town. I always thought Joe did the wrong thing selling it up like that. I would have put a manager out there, while the boys worked under experienced cattle men. That way, when they were a little older and able to run it themselves they would have had a very good station of their own.

Russell began working on his father's roadmaking plant and Glenn, younger than the others and not tied down, went off to South Australia and got himself a job on Kangaroo Island. Some time later, he arrived home with a mate. He'd met Barry Lane on Kangaroo Island and he was fresh out from England. Glenn said to him one weekend, 'I'm going home to see my mum, do you want to come?' He was interested in meeting more Australians, so they picked up their pay, and headed home to Pine Creek.

A very tired and bewildered Barry said to me when they got home, 'I thought he was pulling my leg when I asked him how far away you lived, and he told me it was three thousand miles north!' Barry ended up calling me Mum, and he liked the Territory so much he stayed. He married a Katherine girl and still lives there running a very successful business.

•

NEWS, GOOD OR BAD, always travels fast in the bush. We used to call this miracle the bush telegraph and say that if you cut your finger in the morning the locals had your arm amputated at the shoulder by evening.

I remember one day my girls found a little non-poisonous snake in their birdcage. One of the station owners, who was in the hotel at the time, thought he'd put on a bit of a show for the girls. He went to grab it behind the head. Unfortunately for him, the brew he'd been drinking had messed up his reflexes and the snake bit him between thumb and index finger. His reaction wasn't good. He raced back to the bar for a booster and advice. He got plenty of both.

His mates, under the weather too, tossed up whether to cut it with a razor blade, hack off the arm, take him to Katherine Hospital sixty-four miles down the track, or just sit it out in the bar. They decided on the last course of action. There must have been a news hound passing through as next day, over the radio, we heard 'The station owner bitten by a King Brown snake at the Pine Creek Hotel is in Katherine Hospital, in a serious condition.'

The patient was in Pine Creek alive and kicking and showed no serious after-effects from the snake bite — his major problem was a giant-sized hangover from the 'cure' of too many rums which had been applied by his many bush doctors. I guess you could say the cure was worse than the bite, or, to put it in local lingo, 'If it doesn't cure you, it will bloody well kill you!' The snake itself died of alcoholic poisoning.

The hotel was often the place where people came seeking first-aid. We heard discussion of bush remedies and many yarns of accidents and recoveries, so there was accumulated wisdom in dealing with medical crises. I have seen many an operation performed in the bar.

In the case of snake bite the experts advised, 'a couple of nicks with the old razor blade, suck like hell, and a generous slosh of spirits, and she's a going concern'; for a gash on the skull, 'grab a few hairs on each side of the wound and tie. It's as good as a stitch.' Something in the eye, 'a tongue across the eyeball will shift just about anything!'

One day a chap came into the bar with two black eyes, 'a masterpiece shiner', as one of his mates exclaimed. A bag of black congealed blood hung under each eye. Another mate sat his sorry-looking friend on a stool, peered and poked and walked around looking for the best angle to attack, then produced a razor blade.

My curiosity won, so I moved for a closer look. 'She's a beauty,' I said. 'They don't come any better,' answered the bloke with the razor. The patient peered at me and said, 'Give me a needle, Missus.' (A drink.) I ignored his plea. 'What's the razor blade for?' I asked. 'To lance these bloody things!' 'You can't do that,' I said, but realised they could and would, and that this wouldn't be the first time.

As there was no time to waste, I got to work and produced two 'needles', as I felt both patient and doctor needed a nerve-tightener. As I watched the dark blood run down through the dust and whiskers of the patient's face, I staggered outside and was sick.

I have seen a man poke a red-hot piece of wire into a hollow tooth to kill a nerve when the hole was almost driving him crazy with pain. They all reckoned there was no better place than the pub for the job, as it ensured a quick recovery. At that time, I was the only one in Pine Creek who could provide power and running water. So when the official travelling dental clinic boys came through, they did their work in my small saloon bar, which was situated across the hall from the main bar and joined onto the dining room.

We hung sheets over the glass doors for privacy. In an emergency, they would inject the 'shock absorber' (painkiller) into the gums of the patient, sit and have a couple of beers, and then pull the offending tooth out, still at the bar. When you live in the outback and have toothache, you don't care too much how you get rid of it — as long as it comes out!

On one such occasion, I happened to have a tourist busload in for lunch. As I was serving, I noticed one woman who appeared to be in a state of shock. Following her line of vision, I could understand why. Someone hadn't put the sheet over the door, and there was the man in white, standing over a very fat black girl who was hanging onto the chair for grim death, legs sticking out stiff and straight, mouth red and wide open, while the dentist struggled with a back molar.

In those days we had a lot of fun with the tourists. They were not in a hurry and had time to get to know the folk in the town. The locals loved to show off with a corroboree or 'bullfight' in the bar, or curiosities such as a pond containing small crocodiles, a cocky that gave a lot of cheek, and a jabiru bird that a trucky found on the road one night as a baby. I reared him and called him Junior. He grew into a lovely bird who tried to eat the buttons off your shirt and pecked the girls on the bottom when they bent over. He roamed the hotel and slept outside under a street light standing on one leg. Everyone loved him.

Other little surprises would appear such as a big frilled lizard which pranced along the bar; a python curled up minding its own business on a chair; or a very dead crocodile, mouth wide open, staring out of the cool room!

We had a pony who came in to the bar for a beer and was forever looking over your shoulder when you were working outside; and, at one time, I had a housemaid who owned a little donkey that followed her to work each day. The only place he couldn't go was upstairs.

Tourists would ask me if the locals came in and paid their bills with gold nuggets. Pine Creek has always been known as a gold-mining town, but in all my years in the hotel, the only gold I had seen was alluvial — and no one tried to pass that off on me. So, it was a novelty to find that in the 1980s, with the help of new methods and metal detectors, the men were finding a number of gold nuggets — sometimes large ones — and a few of these have been known to appear in the bar.

I would say the most consistent local face at the hotel had to be, and probably still is, an old miner friend of ours, Darky Dempsey. He originally came from the Riverina in New South Wales, and came to the Territory in 1934. He comes to the hotel nine to five every day of the week, to sit and talk to old friends and make new ones. He knows the country around Pine Creek like the back of his hand. If you are looking for information about a particular place, just ask Darky, he will know, and I'm sure that if he didn't, he would find out for you. He calls himself the local notice board. And the pub is his office. He complained for years that his office chair on the pergola-covered cement out the front of the hotel was open to the elements, and he got wet when it rained. (Readers will be pleased to hear that a covered veranda was later built along the front, and his office is now dry all year round!)

· XII ·

1963–1974: HAZARDS NATURAL AND UNNATURAL

ONCE I HAD the new hotel off and running, I got involved in Pine Creek community activities, as I had done in Katherine. With my children getting older, and as four of them had already left home, I was able to give more time to these things, which I usually found enjoyable and rewarding.

On one such occasion two of our senior ladies had a long-time wish come true when they were baptised. The ceremony took place in our ancient local hall. It was a wet, miserable day, and the Bishop of Carpentaria himself came to officiate. A couple of younger church members were baptised too, and there was quite a roll-up.

The wind blew the rain in through the openings and cracks in the walls. Passing Aborigines poked their heads around the door and giggled, and my girls' pet Pekinese dog followed them to the service, and played with the tassels hanging from the Bishop's robes. It was, nevertheless, a lovely service and the two old ladies, happy now that they had fulfilled their dearest wish, cried in each other's arms.

When a group of men at the Moline Mine suddenly hankered for a round of golf, Pine Creek acquired a golf course. With the help of heavy mining equipment, the miners shifted 50 000 yards of earth and stone, felled trees, filled in gullies and created what must have been the most unusual ironstone golf course in Australia, 190 miles from Darwin and thirty-two miles off the bitumen road at Pine Creek. It had a club house — a little tin shed — built up on a hill overlooking 'the links'. Putting greens were laid. The soles of our shoes were half-fried from the oil in the sifted sand, but the greens were the equal of any on the Darwin course!

Members were divided into working groups, with certain holes to maintain. Despite the tremendous amount of work involved, there would not have been a keener club anywhere. One of the members was so eager to start, he went to Darwin to buy his clubs and hired a plane to fly back. Landing on the third fairway, he hopped out of the plane and managed a few hits to try out the new clubs before dark.

The first time I played I nearly lost my partner. She had landed her ball in a natural hazard: a burned-out tree stump. It took five minutes before the cloud of ashes cleared enough for me to see her after every attempt shot to get out.

According to one of the visitors, the course was sheer hell: although he couldn't really speak with much authority, as he wasn't very often on the fairways during his round. When he hit off, the bitumen-like surface of ironstone ripped his balls, scarred his clubs and jarred his hands, and he didn't find our numerous natural hazards very amusing.

The Moline Golf Club became defunct in later years, but has recently been revived and now has an annual tournament which attracts players from all over the Territory.

On one occasion we organised a vintage car race from Darwin to Katherine. The drivers left Darwin in all sorts of gear: goggles and ancient clothes and hats. Joe and Russell were first over the finishing line but were disqualified, though they continued to claim line honours. It was said that they had installed a fake 'detour' sign on a back road near Mt Todd to confuse the other drivers. I wasn't surprised, knowing Joe's love of practical jokes. Not too many knew those roads as well as he did.

Many of the cars didn't make it back to Katherine, and had to be rescued, and some that did had to be pushed over the finishing line. They were a pretty sorry-looking lot after two hundred-odd very hard miles.

•

IN 1963, a group of local folk keen to have a race meeting in Pine Creek, gathered at the hotel, sat me in a chair, and informed me that I was the President of the newly-formed Pine Creek Race Club. I protested but they said all I had to do was be Lady President and they would do everything else. It didn't take very long to get a committee together and soon we had our first meeting planned. The stations were bringing in their fastest bush horses, and we had a programme with five or six races. The newspapers rang, quite excited, saying I was the only lady president of a race committee that they knew of. What was my knowledge of racehorses? Foolish me, being a bit smart, I said, 'None really, except that one end kicks and the other end bites!' This made big black headlines and left me with egg on my face.

The big crowd which came to town for the races, and for the race ball afterwards, camped on the track with their swags, at the hotel, or just where they fell, and had a great weekend of it in the way of all bush race meetings. Huge fires burned all night, where groups gathered and gossiped, told tall stories and sang songs. Staggering up to the makeshift 'ladies' the next morning, ankle-deep in red dust, and much the worse for wear, you would hear the greeting, 'Come and have a rum, you old bastard!', which could refer to me or anyone else in the vicinity. *This* old bastard had many cups of coffee on the return trip! Breakfast was steak grilled over a fire, and Johnnie cakes made on a shovel or camp oven lid.

Bush race meetings always finished up with the old Aussie game of two-up or swy — illegal of course. A tarpaulin would be spread out on the grass down in the scrub and the light determined the length of the game. If the arm of the law gave them a fair go, and attended to other police matters, a few hurricane lamps were brought in. As it only involved one night a year, and if it was trouble-free, they usually got away with it.

In those days, if mates disagreed about something and had a bloody good fight, they shook hands afterwards, and then went back to the boozer. If a few of the younger ones played up, whatever their colour, they got a boot up the bum, and were sent on their way.

For all the station folk the bush meeting became the big event of the season. Everyone came, along with horses, dogs and kids for a long weekend in town. The stockmen, who were too far out of town to have weekends off, would make up for it in these few days, having a big spend-up and packing in as much socialising and fun as they possibly could. The Aboriginal stockmen would wear their best ringer gear, sporting flash boots and hats, and their girls had nice new dresses that the missus had made for them.

At one of these meetings, one ringer had managed to have a sip of someone's 'pflagon' of plonk, and so he went looking for his wife to get some more money. She replied 'Me no more gottim money'. He insisted, 'And might be you gottim longa skirt pocket!' 'No.' She stuck her hands in her pockets and they came out empty. 'Might be you gottim longa shirt pocket?' To convince him, she took off her shirt and flapped it in the air in front of him. Then, she whipped off her skirt and did the same thing. 'See,' she yelled, getting into the swing of things, 'Me no more bin gottim.' By this time she was jumping up and down flapping her arms, stark naked. She was gathering a large crowd of onlookers, and enjoying the show herself. 'You gottim,' her husband growled, although by now his hopes were getting low. 'What'sa matter belonga you?' she cried out, 'Might be you think me gottim up this arse 'ole belonga me!'

The voice of the law fortunately brought things to a halt at this point. 'You pair want to go to the races?' he asked. 'Youi,' they agreed. 'Well get your clothes on,' he said to the stripteaser, 'and get going or you will both spend your weekend in the lock-up.'

The race meetings and most of our social events were held in the dry season, because when the wet comes between November and April, there is not much else to do but find a veranda, and wait for the weather to rain itself out. The hotel proved to be one of the most popular verandas in the district during the wet!

●

THE WET SEASON never had any adverse effect on me. I really loved that time of the year: just to lie in bed and listen to the rain hitting the old tin roof was joy in itself. It doesn't thrill everyone to listen to the thunder and watch the lightning, but I always felt refreshed and renewed by it, and enjoyed the dramatic beauty of the deep purple skies, spiked with electric flashes of lightning. The countryside took on a lush green look, the rain washed the red dust off the trees, rocks and buildings, and settled the roads, and my garden thrived, and the cane grass grew head high.

Activities are virtually at a standstill for the three months or so of the wet, as few roads are passable. There are swarms of flies and mosquitoes; it's hard to read in the evenings as every creepy crawly seems attracted to the light and flying ants lose their wings and crawl all over the place. The stink, or lavender beetles leave their dreadful smell everywhere, a steaming heat rises from the earth after every shower of rain, and the humidity gets so high you feel you could carve the air with a knife. The sweat just pours out of your skin. All of which depresses some people, and they sometimes go 'troppo'.

These folk are usually people experiencing the tropics for the first time. A young geologist who had come up to take on a surveying job out from Pine Creek, was one victim. The combined pressures of the isolation, the rough camp conditions and the oppressive heat just got too much for him. A young couple who were travelling down to Katherine in their little Volkswagen were amazed when a crazed-looking man jumped out onto the road ahead of them, stark naked, and flagged down their car. They slowed, but decided they would not risk picking him up. As they passed him, he jumped on to the bonnet of their car, and with a branch of a tree he was carrying started to belt the hell out of it. The driver, terrified, accelerated and their attacker flew off into the mud on the side of the road. They raced back to town, and came into the pub to report a madman who, they reckoned, qualified for a straight jacket!

The fellow was later 'rescued' by the police, and made a hasty return trip to the south.

Over the years we had the odd serious fight, and a couple of shootings and stabbings. Usually the offenders were outsiders who came into town, hit the grog and became aggressive — often over a woman. In 1963, however, a local fellow stabbed another to death in Pine Creek, and headed out to the bush. The police staged what they said was the biggest manhunt ever mounted in the Territory. Police on horseback, on foot and with radio-equipped vehicles covered thousands of miles. Road blocks were built, trains and transports searched. Interstate police were alerted, but reports of sightings of the man always came to dead ends when followed up by the police. It was generally accepted that he had died in the bush. About a year later, the fellow, who had been living in the bush outside Darwin, got fed up, and gave himself up to the police. I had known him for a long time, and always thought of him as a nice clean gentleman. He was the last person I would have imagined in this situation.

The train still came through Pine Creek, although it didn't stay overnight any more, and the railway boys were still regular customers of the hotel during the brief stop. On one trip, returning to Darwin from Katherine, the guard and driver hatched a plan. To increase the time to get over to the hotel and back, the driver would slow down just outside Pine Creek, allowing the guard to jump out, run over to the hotel, duck in for a dozen bottles of beer, then sprint down to the station in time to catch the train as it pulled out. Unfortunately, on one occasion the driver forgot to slow down at the usual spot; being thirsty, the guard jumped anyway and broke his arm. I thought it would have been most interesting to find out what excuse for the accident was given to the railway authorities.

We had some odd local characters. One loved to sneak a nip of metho out of the jars kept on the bar counter which held preserved snakes. There were many yarns told of blokes like this. When they were out in the bush, they drank metho mixed with water and, on special occasions, added a dash of Eno's Fruit Salts to make Bushman's Champagne.

Some of these lonely old bushmen who were habitual boozers, resorted to all sorts of odd potions when out on their own and continued to use the cheaper brews when in town. Disinfectant wasn't safe to leave around, and I heard talk of strychnine in water as a great bucker-upper: it was said that one old man would wet the tip of his penknife on his tongue, dip it in a bottle of strychnine tap the blade on the neck of the bottle, then lick the poison off the blade. He would give a bit of a shudder, and then take off on a 'high'.

Little Joe Fahey, who knew he had a bad heart, came back to Pine Creek to die, as he wished. Little Joe had been a close friend of ours from pre-war days. He worked in the construction and building trades in the area. He was a frequent visitor to our house over the years, and when the children were small always arrived with a big bag of lollies for them. They loved Uncle Joe! He was a very friendly and likeable character, and that is why the community thought so highly of him. It was said that he had made all the crosses for the war graves at Adelaide River.

When the sad day came, we applied for him to be buried in the town cemetery, but the district officer in Katherine said that as our cemetery is by law no cemetery at all, it would be no more legal to bury him there than to bury him by the side of the Stuart Highway.

We were all so determined that Joe would have this last wish fulfilled, that we took the matter to Tiger Brennan, then the member for Victoria River, and he persuaded the bureaucrats that it was fit and right to bury him at Pine Creek. There was no worry getting helpers to dig his grave. Father Thomas Pius Ormonde came down from Darwin to bury his old friend, and the last prayers were held in the court house, as we had no Catholic Church. It was right that the pub should have closed for the morning; after all, he had built it.

•

IN 1963, Joe purchased Bonrook Station which was just a few miles out of Pine Creek. The homestead was in a very poor state, so he built a nice new one and put in a bore and overhead tank. He and Warren did a lot of clearing and put in miles of fencing. If there was ten miles to the crinkly on a Beenleigh rum bottle, no doubt you would have measured the stubbies and tinnies to the post holes or tractor miles during the improvements at Bonrook.

There was a lovely swimming hole in the creek in front of the homestead. One day when I went out to visit the boys, one of the blacks sang out to me, 'Hey, Missus, that one Freddie Woods he bin cum up.' Fred was licensee of the Commercial Hotel in Katherine at the time. I raced inside, whipped my apron off, brushed my hair, and tried to make myself look a bit respectable for visitors, but no Fred Woods turned up. When I asked the fellow where Fred had got to, he replied, 'He bin sit down longa that one water hole.' I found out that Freddie Woods was an old bull that Joe had nicknamed after his mate in Katherine!

One thing I will always remember about Bonrook was the toilet. I have described some classics already, but this had to be seen to be believed: hessian stretched around a few trees for privacy, and a long slit trench with forked posts at each end. The forked posts supported a pole, which went over the trench for people to sit on, and there was another set of posts supporting a pole in front of the hole for holding on to. It wasn't easy to handle the apparel, cling to one set of rails and squat over the other. To negotiate the paper was a work of art!

I never lived on any of the stations for any length of time, but my visits to Bonrook, and to other station homesteads, made me realise what a wonderful way of life it was. Some might think that life on a remote Territory cattle station would be dull and boring, but there was always plenty to do: housework, meals, animals to attend to, and always a garden with flowers and vegetables to look after. And you had plenty of company, as the stations were almost like small towns in themselves in those days, with the manager, bookkeeper, and stockmen's families, and usually a big blacks' camp.

Unfortunately, during the time the boys were running the cattle stations, I had little chance of enjoying that part of their lives with them. I was between a rock and a hard place, running the hotel to keep finances up to help out and keep the home fires burning. So, sadly, I had only a few brief stays out bush.

The isolation of Pine Creek didn't affect any of us until the girls reached the end of primary school. There was no choice except to send them off to boarding school, and as I had already been through this with the boys, I dreaded the thought of it. I chose to send Leonie to Charters Towers, in western Queensland, with two of her girlfriends, Kay and Sue Scott, from Katherine.

To get to Charters Towers it was a day's car journey to Darwin, where they could catch a plane. This went to Mt Isa, where the girls had to stay overnight. We arranged for them to be met by a Church of England minister and his wife, who looked after them and put them on the plane which flew them to Townsville on the Queensland coast. From there they were taken by bus to Charters Towers.

Leonie was not only homesick, but airsick and carsick as well. So, I finally brought her back to the Uniting Church school in Darwin, close to home, where I could visit her more often. She and another little girl from Pine Creek were the only white girls boarding at the school. They had a room at the teachers' residence. When the other girl got sick, it was found that she had leprosy — the first white child in the Territory, I believe, to contract the disease. After this, I brought Leonie home. She had no mind to return to school and, as she was fifteen, she started work helping me at the hotel.

When it was time for Sandra and Susanne to go away for secondary schooling, I decided to send them to boarding school in Adelaide. It was nine hours on the plane from Katherine in those days, and the trip was called the milk run, as it stopped all along the way with mail and cargo. The girls settled well in Adelaide, and were well cared for, but it was always tears when they were leaving, tears while they were away, tears when they came home. Joe said that he never met a woman who howled as much as I did!

In 1965, I decided to lease the Pine Creek Hotel for five years, so I could go to Adelaide and stay there until the two younger girls finished their education. Leonie came down to live with us too, and it gave her a chance to work in a big city and see a bit more of the world. At first, it was hard to settle to the inactivity of just being a house person, but I made myself busy. The five years I was away from Pine Creek, from 1965 to 1970, seemed like a lifetime. Thankfully, the couple who'd leased the hotel did a good job and kept things going. But I couldn't get back north quickly enough. The hotel was the meeting place of all my friends, there was always company, and I shared the joys and sorrows of my community. The feeling of being there whenever someone wanted a friend to celebrate with, or needed a shoulder to cry on or just to talk to — it all added up to belonging. It was my way of life, and there wasn't anywhere else I wanted to be.

I felt really warmed by the welcome home I received. The *Northern Territory Times* gave me a surprise. When I opened it one day, I saw a paragraph headed in bold black type: **MAYSE YOUNG COMES HOME**. That's how I felt and will always feel about Pine Creek — it's home.

Susie stayed in Adelaide to work, and Sandra, who hadn't found any career which suited her better than the hotel, came back to work with me at Pine Creek. Leonie had married her trucky boyfriend, Bill Ruig, and was living in Port Lincoln, South Australia; Glenn had gone to live in Darwin with his wife Pam; Warren and Russell both had small children, and were living at Bonrook and Pine Creek. Marlene was settled in Darwin, with her husband Tom Atkinson, and five children. Joe, by this time had moved to Darwin, and was still working some of his roadmaking plant.

In 1971, Susanne, my youngest girl, her husband, Paul Smith and myself purchased the Katherine

Hotel (my old rival) from one of the grandchildren of the O'Sheas, who had been such good friends to my parents. The three of us went to live in Katherine, to run the hotel and build up the business. Susanne was becoming very competent as a hotel owner and manager.

We made a success of the Katherine Hotel. Then, in 1973, the Northern Territory Brewing Company offered us the lease of the Seabreeze Hotel at Nightcliff in Darwin. We were there like a shot out of a gun. We loved the idea of going to live in Darwin, to enjoy the change of living right on the sea.

We installed managers in both the Katherine and Pine Creek Hotels, allowing us to move to Darwin and enjoy the Seabreeze. It was a lovely tropical hotel, with an uninterrupted view of the Arafura Sea, and had a real family atmosphere. We had comfortable accommodation set in beautiful grounds with a swimming pool and a beer garden and often had pool parties, barbecues and bingo for entertainment at the hotel.

In late November 1974, a solid wet set in. We looked forward to the Christmas period, the off season for tourists, when things would be very quiet around the Seabreeze, giving us time to relax. By then I had fourteen grandchildren, and was already a great-grandmother. It was the beginning of a new period in my life. After looking after a household and children with one hand, and running a business with another for over thirty years, I might at last take life a little easier. I was still working at the Seabreeze, of course, but I was sharing the responsibilities with the girls and it felt luxurious to be near the sea and all the shops and amenities of Darwin.

· XIII ·

1974: NO QUIET RETIREMENT

1974 WAS GOING TO BE a really special Christmas. It was our first by the sea in Darwin again since my children were all little, and we were planning a big Christmas Day get-together at the Seabreeze Hotel. The whole family had gathered in Darwin. The only one who would not be with us was Warren, who had stayed with his family in the little shop they were running near the Pine Creek Hotel.

Before we could enjoy our own celebrations, however, Marlene, Sandra and Susanne and my son-in-laws Bob and Paul and I had customers to look after on Christmas Eve. A large group had booked the barbecue area for their Christmas party. The barbecue was out by the pool and the few downpours of warm heavy rain during the evening didn't dampen their spirits at all. The pool had a sun roof over it and most of the guests were suitably attired in their bathers anyway.

There had been a strong wind warning on the news and a cyclone was reported to have passed us by. Cyclone Selma had been near Darwin without any ill-effects a few weeks before, so the standard pre-recorded radio message about Cyclone Tracy did not raise any particular alarm.

As the evening wore on, however, the winds got stronger and stronger, and around eleven most people went home. Then, to our surprise, two weary travellers pulled in and booked a room — they had come from Kalgoorlie in Western Australia. Sandra, Bob and their children stayed with me at the Seabreeze, and Sue and Marlene drove off to their own homes for the night.

By 11.30 pm the winds were so strong that the iron roof started to lift off the breezeway built between the hotel and the accommodation units. The cyclone had suddenly picked up strength from the warm waters of the Arafura Sea, just off Bathurst Island, and changed course — heading straight back to Darwin. We had no warning, but the howling winds and crashing iron of the roof meant that there was no way anyone could get to sleep. We sat together waiting for the storm to ease.

Sandra's children had been the only ones who had gone to bed that night. About the time the breezeway was ripped off the main roof by the wind, I moved their mattresses away from the windows, into the walk-in dressing room — and I was later immensely relieved I had done so, as those windows were the first to go. They exploded inwards with the noise of a bomb, and sprayed shards of glass everywhere. By then the power station had cut out, and the city was in complete darkness.

•

BY MIDNIGHT we saw the breezeway had been completely blown apart, and we could hear the main roof starting to lift. Bob made it over to the room of our only guests — the exhausted couple from Kalgoorlie — and told them to grab their belongings and stay in their bathroom. It was the safest place, we decided, as it was reinforced by the pipes structured through the walls. Only a few yards away Sandra, Bob, their children and I all huddled together inside the manager's flat. We were in pitch darkness and the force of the wind, exploding glass and flying debris made such a noise that we could not communicate with them.

As the storm raged on we were surprised to see Russell, soaked through and sheltering his baby in his arms. His wife Margaret, holding their other small child, was close behind him. Over the noise of the wind, they explained in fragmented shouts that their holiday caravan had been smashed in by a tree. In the darkness they had to walk the several hundred yards over to the hotel. It was incredible that they reached us unhurt.

Then to our amazement Sue and her husband Paul called out in the darkness, and groped their way into our makeshift shelter of mattresses. They had endured a terrifying drive through the storm, but when their stilt house at Nightcliff began rocking, they knew they had to find somewhere safer. As they drove, the rain was blinding and they had to guess where the road was from memory. A flash of lightning saved their lives when it illuminated their way for a moment, and they realised their car was driving directly at the cliff and certain death. They were very shaken. I wondered helplessly how all my other children were.

I had experienced cyclones as a child in northern Queensland, but never like this. Every once-secure barrier between us and the wind was fast falling away like matchwood. Too late, we realised we should have moved everyone over to the hotel freezer room. It was built of concrete. But by then, it would have been foolhardy to move even those few yards. We tried to talk confidently, and even sang songs and told the children stories from time to time. We took it in turns to hold the two babies and the other children quietly snuggled in tight, trusting us to keep them safe.

Shouting at each other over the noise, we decided that the walls next to the toilet and kitchen were probably the safest, so we inched our group across the floor, holding pillows and mattresses over the children to protect them from the flying glass and razor-sharp sheets of iron. Although we were knee-deep in water by then, we put mattresses up against all openings, and boxed ourselves into the remains of a small hallway. There were now twelve of us and five dogs, who cringed in against us, terrified. When they could, the men grabbed pieces of timber or steel to shaft through the fibro cement walls and ceiling, for extra support.

After eight hours of the cyclone, we were all totally exhausted. At dawn, the winds started to abate. I looked at my family — all dazed, bedraggled and wet as drowned rats, but thankfully unharmed. I had an agonising wait, until one by one the others all made their way to us at the Seabreeze.

Leonie had stayed at Fannie Bay with friends. She told us they went to bed at about 11.30 pm then woke when the walls started to leave the house, which was up on stilts, like many Darwin houses. They all rushed downstairs and huddled in a brick and cement room — a recent addition to the house. It saved their lives. The next morning the house, like all those in the street, was a pile of rubble.

Leonie's reaction was typically pragmatic. At daylight, she and her boyfriend, Doug, managed to borrow a four-wheel drive vehicle that was still intact, and set out to search for her family. It was slow going, but the four-wheel drive was able to get through the streets clogged with uprooted trees and rubbish.

The first person they saw was a man with one arm almost ripped off — the skin and flesh just hung as if he had been savaged by a wild animal. They threw a mattress on to the back of the truck, and drove him to the Moil school, which was being set up as a community shelter. She saw people coming out from wrecked houses, shocked and exhausted. She assisted where she could, helping people who were trying to carry their injured relatives to safety and medical attention.

The sight of Glenn and Pam's flattened house

frightened her; she thought they must all be dead. But by this time the family had scrambled their way out, and were sitting in a car in a state of shock.

Joe, my husband, was spending the evening with friends out in one of the Casuarina suburbs. By the time the full blast hit Darwin, they were well into the Christmas celebrations. Once the roof and walls of the house started to give way, Joe grabbed a blanket and jumped into a big bath tub — his friends lay on the floor downstairs. In the morning Joe bellowed down the drain pipe 'Are you all right?' 'Yes. You OK?' they yelled back. This sort of communication went on for a while, until he sat up in his tub, and they got up from the floor. When they found out they were in fact all in the same room they couldn't stop laughing.

Leonie reported that when she arrived to check on him, he was sitting on the top of the stairs, no walls around him, drinking beer. 'Trust Dad to relax with a beer at a time like that!' she commented dryly.

•

AFTER WE LOOKED over the Seabreeze, we realised we had to set to work. Our most urgent need was fresh water, as all the water pipes and sewage system had been destroyed. We set out as many buckets and containers as we could find to catch the rainwater each time another downpour began. The kitchen of the hotel was a complete write-off, so I had the men set up a portable stove with a gas bottle which I spotted amongst the wreckage. We made a few makeshift tables and chairs, and set up a place where I could prepare and serve meals. The fresh food was unusable; luckily we had plenty of tinned stuff.

In the hot sunny periods we hung out all the bedding we could find and the men worked on making what was left of the flats into temporary accommodation. We dug trenches in the lawn and piled all the rotting Christmas food and sodden debris into them. By Christmas afternoon, a rotting stench pervaded the whole of Darwin. Leonie's boyfriend Doug managed to find a generator, which he rigged up to make us a lighting plant, and by evening, we were managing quite well.

By Boxing Day we had things well organised, and felt ready to offer assistance to others. We decided we could probably help most by functioning as a centre for meals and refreshments for some of the volunteer teams and police boys — who were by now working in groups, still rescuing people, clearing wreckage, and piling up and burning the hundreds of animal carcasses which had washed up on the beach. Word soon got around and we had a continual stream of exhausted people calling in for a meal and a short rest.

Assistance from the Federal Government emergency services was slow in coming. For those first few days, Darwin people coped alone; they quickly organised themselves and volunteer groups worked for long hours on the most urgent jobs of rescue and providing temporary shelter and food for the many who found themselves homeless. Many of the volunteers did not sleep for two days.

The police had the terrible job of trying to trace the lost, recovering bodies, and identifying the dead. Because of the lack of power, and the humid tropical conditions, all bodies were photographed, a description taken, and then they had to be hastily buried. There were queues of distraught people lining up at the police depots to view the photographs. It was a terrible way to find a lost relative or friend.

All stray animals had to be destroyed, because of the fear that they might start eating decayed flesh and perhaps start a plague. A shudder went through me every time I heard a shot ring out. To people living in the outback, a dog was truly man's best friend.

During the week after Tracy, I had only been out of the Seabreeze for one short look around our neighbourhood. Driving out to the airport on New Year's

Eve, for the first time I realised that an entire city was destroyed. It was like losing an old friend. The Darwin I had known for most of my life, was gone. If I had been able to find some kind of work to do to help restore her, I would have felt a lot better. In some ways, the toehold we made in the ruin of the Seabreeze had helped us come to terms with Tracy. Leaving Darwin was the moment we finally acknowledged to ourselves that it was all gone.

The airport itself had received a lot of damage. Small aircraft were wrapped around trees and buildings, or lying on their sides on the tarmac. The waiting room was partly blown away and water was lying in huge puddles from the rain leaking through the roof. Glenn, who worked at the airport, warned us of the crowds of people, mostly women and children, waiting in the heat. Exhausted and bedraggled, we joined them and waited hours for a signal to board the Hercules plane.

The future now loomed frighteningly blank. It had been difficult enough to come to grips with the present. I had always tried to teach my children to look ahead, and felt now that I could not show any fear or weakness at this crucial point. It would have helped to have had a clear next step for us, but there was none. We had virtually no possessions, no cash, and nowhere to go. We would have to accept the assistance of the Red Cross in Adelaide, and take it day by day. This was the second Christmas in my life that I had sat at this airport with my family, forced to leave Darwin, with just a few salvaged belongings.

But it is times like this that your whole life, your whole world, takes on a different perspective and the mind sees things in a clear sharp way. I felt very glad to be alive, and overwhelmingly grateful to know that my family were safe and had survived unharmed. They were the most precious thing in my life and, knowing this, the loss of our possessions did not seem so important at all.

I thought of my mother, and once again, her words came back to me:

'Material things can be replaced', she had said. And they were.

POSTSCRIPT

M AYSE AND *her family did return to Darwin, as soon as they were allowed after the government clean-up.*

The Northern Territory Breweries had the remains of the original Seabreeze Hotel demolished. Sadly, it was never rebuilt, and the site was sold.

Her youngest daughter, Susanne, now owns the Pine Creek Hotel, and runs it with her husband, Chris Mason, and sisters Marlene, Sandra and brother-in-law, Bob Holmes.

Leonie now owns the original Pine Creek Hotel building which she renovated and has made her home. She does relief work at the Pine Creek Hotel for her sisters, as well as working in the district tourist industry.

Glenn lives and works in Darwin, Russell in Pine Creek and Warren on a cattle property in Queensland.

Mayse still owns shares in the Katherine Hotel, and has joined Susanne, Sandra and their husbands in the ownership of the Seaview Motel-Restaurant, which overlooks Fannie Bay in Darwin. They have renamed it the Seabreeze. Mayse, now retired, divides her time between her many children, grandchildren and great-grandchildren — all of whom proudly consider themselves Territorians.

Jim Dowling, Mayse's brother, still owns and runs the Parap Hotel in Darwin, with his sons Terry and Allan.

Joe (Bogger) Young died in Darwin in 1983.

Beatrice, long-time friend and helper of the Young family, married in Darwin after the war and had a daughter whom she named after Mayse. Her husband was killed in an accident working for the Highways Department. Beatrice devoted herself to caring for children in the Darwin Aboriginal community and worked for some years in the Katherine Hospital laundry. She was awarded the OBE for her work with Aboriginal children and died in the Katherine Hospital in 1986.